HEALTHY GUT
COOKBOOK

150 STAGE-BY-STAGE HEALING RECIPES
to **improve** your **digestive health**

GAVIN PRITCHARD, RDN, CSSD, CD-N, CDE,
AND
MAYA GANGADHARAN, NTP

Contents

UNDERSTANDING GUT HEALTH   8

When Digestion Goes Wrong   10
The Five R's of Gut Healing   12
Pillars of the Diet   14

THE HEALTHY GUT DIET   16

What to Expect   18
Preparing Yourself   20
Preparing Your Kitchen and Pantry   22
Planning Ahead   24
Stage 1 Intro Diet   26
Stage 1 Meal Plan   28
Stage 2 Intro Diet   30
Stage 2 Meal Plan   32
Stage 3 Intro Diet   34
Stage 3 Meal Plan   36
Stage 4 Intro Diet   38
Stage 4 Meal Plan   40
Stage 5 Intro Diet   42
Stage 5 Meal Plan   44

Stage 6 Intro Diet   46
Stage 6 Meal Plan   48
The Full Diet   50
The Full Diet Meal Plan   52
Going Forward   54

FOUNDATION RECIPES AND BASICS   56

Meat Stock   58
Chicken Stock   59
Beef Bone Broth   60
Fermenting Basics   62
Red Cabbage Kraut   64
Fermented Mixed Vegetables   66
Cultured Spring Vegetables   67
Home-Churned Butter   68
Ghee   70
Nut Milk   71
Cultured Dairy Basics   72
Yogurt   74
Cultured Cream   76
Kefir   77
Everyday Grain-Free Bread   78

RECIPES BY STAGE   80

Stage 1   82

Classic Chicken Soup   84
Butternut Squash Soup   85
Carrot Beetroot Soup   86
Chicken Vegetable Soup   88
Garlicky Greens Soup   89
Sweet-and-Sour Chicken Vegetable Soup   90
Summer Garden Soup   92
Three-Onion Soup   93
Pumpkin Bisque   94
Creamy Tomato Soup   96
Greek Lemon Vegetable Soup   97
Beetroot and Beef Short Rib Borscht   98
Stewed Beef Porridge   100
Lemon Peppercorn Poached Chicken Breast   101
Pan Steak with Mushrooms   102

Stage 2   104

Egg Drop Soup   106
Vegetable Beef Stewp   107
Braised Beef Burgers   108
Asian Braised Turkey Meatballs   110
Chicken-Stuffed Cabbage Rolls   111
Chicken Vegetable Ratatouille   112
Chicken Enchilada Casserole   114
Lemon Rosemary Salmon   115
Braised Tomato Sage Turkey Legs   116

Stage 3   118

Sauerkraut Scramble   120
Santa Fe Breakfast Tostadas   121
Asparagus Fried Eggs   122
Roasted Butternut Squash   124
    Pancakes
Easy Avocado Omelette   125
Aromatic Chicken   126
    with Mushrooms

Stage 4   128

Ginger Pumpkin Muffins   130
Chicken Muffins   131
Green Goddess Juice   132
Peppery Pear Juice   132
Liver-Loving Juice   133
Garlic Chicken with Vegetables   134
Grilled Salmon with Walnut Pesto   135
"Spaghetti" with Pomodoro Sauce   136
Oven-Roasted Turkey Meatloaf   138
Classic Pot Roast with Onions   139
Minced Beef Stroganoff   140
Minced Beef Empanadas   142
Crackling Nuts   143

Stage 5   144

Simple House Salad   146
Grain-Free Tabbouleh   147
Mini Butternut Squash Soufflés   148
Guacamole   150
Easy Chicken Stir-Fry   151
Tex-Mex Pulled Pork Burritos   152
Apple Pie Stewed Apples   154
Baked Cinnamon Walnut   155
    Apples

Stage 6   156

Anytime Smoothies   158
Roasted Brussels   159
    Sprout Apple Salad
Scallops Piccata   160
Olive Raisin Tapenade   162
Chicken Thigh Puttanesca   163
Dairy-Free Key Lime Mousse   164
Seasonal Mixed-Berry Crostata   166
Honey Bombs   168
Gingered Vanilla Honey Drops   169

Full Diet   170

Honey Sage Sausage Patties   172
Sausage, Egg, and   173
    Cheese Sandwich
Cheddar Chive Biscuits   174
Grainless Granola   176
Grilled Vegetable Frittata   177
Chopped Cobb Salad   178
Calming Kale Salad   180
Grilled Steak Salad   181
Seared Scallop Salad   182
    with Asian Vegetables
Wedge Salad with Ranch   184
Spring Tuna Niçoise Salad   185
Salmon Spinach Cobb Salad   186
Chunky Chicken Salad   188
Chicken Cheddar Sandwiches   190
Turkey Reubens   191
Lamb Burger Sliders   192
Margherita Pizza   194
Tuna Cakes with Rémoulade   195
Oven-Roasted Moroccan Chicken   196
Slammin' Hot Slaw   198
Tiger Prawn and Cauliflower Grits   199
Kimchi   200
Cauliflower Hummus   202

Garden Fresh Salsa   203
Tzatziki Sauce   203
Parmesan Rosemary Tuiles   204
Three-Seed Crackers   206
Nut Butter   208
Nut Cheese   209
Spiced Carrot Cake   210
Hunger Buster Bars   211
Very Berry "Ice Cream"   212
Lemon Almond Flour Biscotti   214

Index of Recipes by Type   216
Index   218

Introduction

We've all heard phrases referencing the relationship between your innards and your emotions, such as "gut feelings". Recently, medical professionals have begun to explore the connection between your gut and your health.

Leaky Gut Syndrome

Recent studies have linked the microbiome — another word for the world of friendly (and sometimes unfriendly) bacteria and microbes that live in your intestines — to weight loss, depression, Alzheimer's disease, autism, and more. Problems like gas, bloating, constipation, and diarrhoea are often thought of as normal, but in fact they are often symptoms of a "leaky gut" that has become compromised by stress, bad habits, bad food choices, or toxins. It's best to correct the problem before deeper issues develop.

The GAPS Diet

This book focuses on a gut-healing protocol called the Gut and Psychology Syndrome™, or GAPS, diet. The GAPS diet was created to address specific physical and physiological gut-related health issues. This book was written and designed to make this somewhat complicated protocol easier to understand and implement, and to give you more recipe options.

Based on the Specific Carbohydrate Diet (SCD), the GAPS diet was developed by neurologist and nutritionist Dr Natasha Campbell-McBride. Her book **Gut and Psychology Syndrome** outlines the science of the protocol, and we recommend reading it to understand in detail how the gut becomes unbalanced and why the diet works. You also can visit gapsdiet.com for more information. There you can find a certified GAPS practitioner if you decide you want a bit more guidance.

Other Related Diets

Several other diets share similarities with the GAPS diet and are used to treat health issues that stem from the gut. Like GAPS, the Paleo diet focuses on reducing carbohydrates, avoiding grains and refined sugar, and increasing nutrient-dense whole foods. One of the ways it differs from GAPS is that it does not allow dairy products. The low-FODMAP diet is another protocol for gut healing that focuses on eliminating particular carbohydrates, such as certain sugars. One way it differs from GAPS is in the list of allowed foods. Because you might be incorporating elements of other diets with the GAPS diet, we include icons with the recipes to denote whether they are compatible with the Paleo or low-FODMAP diet.

The Basics of Healing

In **Healthy Gut Cookbook,** we begin with an overview of how digestion is supposed to work and what can go wrong. We also give you the basics of both the healing process and the diet itself, as well as offering advice on how to prepare your kitchen and pantry for a healthy gut. From there, we walk you through each stage of the introduction diet, from Stage 1 to Stage 6, and explain how to transition to the full GAPS diet. Don't skip over this part; you'll want to be familiar with each stage and what you can expect before you begin.

ICONS

Throughout the recipes, you'll see various icons. Here's what they mean:

PEANUT- AND NUT-FREE RECIPE This icon denotes recipes that are free of peanuts and tree nuts.

NUT FREE

DAIRY-FREE RECIPE This icon indicates recipes that do not require animal-sourced dairy products.

DAIRY FREE

PALEO-FRIENDLY RECIPE This icon indicates recipes that are suitable for those who are also following the Paleo diet.

PALEO DIET

LOW-FODMAP RECIPE This icon denotes recipes that are acceptable for readers also following the low-FODMAP diet.

LOW FODMAP

Allergies and Sensitivities

Leaky gut syndrome can cause allergic reactions and intolerances to particular food types. Not everyone has the same allergies and intolerances, so we include icons to flag the recipes that do not contain nuts or dairy, the two food groups most commonly reacted to. If you are unsure of your intolerances, we provide instructions for two common tests in the "Going Forward" section. As your gut heals, you may be able to reintroduce dairy, and we provide steps for doing that in the same section.

The Path to Feeling Better

Most people notice positive results within the first couple of stages. Those with deeper healing issues might have to wait a little longer, or you might need subsequent rounds of the introduction diet to complete the healing process. Although the first few stages are restricted, the later stages and the full GAPS diet are full of delicious possibilities that not only taste good, but also help support vibrant health. Good luck on your journey!

Healing in Stages

The diet is very specific about what foods can be eaten when, so the recipes are organized by stage, indicated by an icon. Be sure to follow the diet strictly. Don't add foods earlier than they're allowed, or you risk compromising your healing. You can always go back to earlier recipes after you've moved onto the next stage.

Stage 1 Focuses on stocks, boiled meats, some well-cooked vegetables, and cultured dairy.

Stage 4 Allows roasted and baked meats and fish, fresh juices, and some seed and nut flours.

Stage 2 Allows the addition of raw egg yolks, stews, herbs, and ghee.

Stage 5 Reintroduces apples, raw vegetables in salads, fruit juice, spices, and other nut flours.

Stage 3 Allows you to add avocado, cooked eggs, asparagus, and a few other vegetables.

Stage 6 Allows more raw fruits, Brazil nuts, and more sweet baked goods.

Full diet This is the maintenance phase, which allows greater variety but continues to restrict some foods.

Understanding Gut Health

When things go wrong in your gut, it affects the rest of your body, as well as your mind. In this part, you learn about leaky gut syndrome, and how the right diet can put you on the path to healing.

When Digestion Goes Wrong

Leaky gut syndrome occurs when the lining of the small intestine becomes too permeable, causing a cascade of immune responses that can lead to chronic health problems. This permeability can be due to inflammatory foods such as gluten, dairy, sugar, and alcohol; some medications; intestinal parasites; and even stress.

1 Brain

- **NORMAL FUNCTION** Digestion actually begins in the brain, when you see, smell, or sometimes even think of food. Your mouth begins to water, and your body begins to prepare the various digestive organs to receive and process food.

- **WHAT CAN GO WRONG** This step of digestion can go wrong when you're eating under stress – in the car, during a meeting, or while doing chores – which puts your body in fight-or-flight rather than rest-and-digest mode, and hampers the digestive process from the very beginning.

2 Mouth

- **NORMAL FUNCTION** In the mouth, food is broken down mechanically by chewing and chemically by enzymes present in saliva.

- **WHAT CAN GO WRONG** If you gulp down your food instead of chewing it properly, you force your stomach to do more work. This puts stress on your digestive system and can result in food being improperly digested.

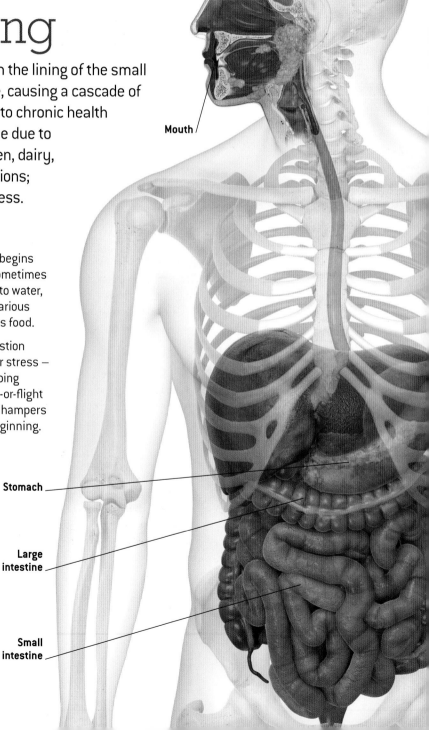

Brain

Mouth

Stomach

Large intestine

Small intestine

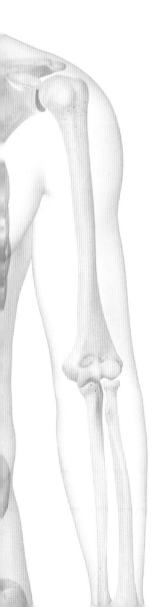

3 Stomach

- **NORMAL FUNCTION** Your stomach breaks down food mechanically by contracting the muscles of the stomach wall, and chemically using stomach acid and digestive enzymes.

- **WHAT CAN GO WRONG** It's very common for a person to underproduce (rather than overproduce, as commonly believed) stomach acid, which can lead to problems like heartburn and acid reflux, and contribute to leaky gut and food allergies.

4 Small Intestine

- **NORMAL FUNCTION** The small intestine is where most of the digestion of nutrients takes place. The lining of the small intestine is designed to be permeable so that properly digested food can be absorbed into the bloodstream and lymphatic system and circulated around the body.

- **WHAT CAN GO WRONG** Leaky gut occurs when the lining becomes too permeable, allowing undigested food particles, toxins, and microbes into the bloodstream, where the body attacks them as foreign invaders.

5 Large Intestine

- **NORMAL FUNCTION** A small amount of nutrient absorption occurs in the large intestine. In addition, the large intestine reabsorbs water from the food, and beneficial bacteria in the large intestine convert waste into nutrients before the food is expelled as faeces.

- **WHAT CAN GO WRONG** If you're dehydrated, your large intestine will hold faeces as your body tries to reabsorb as much water as possible, causing constipation. If there are not enough beneficial bacteria in the colon, opportunistic bacteria can overwhelm the environment, causing gut dysbiosis.

LEAKY GUT SYNDROME

Leaky gut is believed to cause many physical and physiological issues. Stress, diet, inflammation, candida, and zinc deficiency are all considered possible causes.

HEALTHY GUT

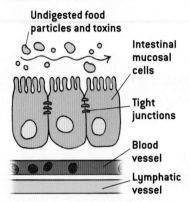

Healthy gut Junctions between mucosal cells lining the small intestine are tight and do not allow toxins to reach the bloodstream.

LEAKY GUT

Leaky gut It is believed junctions become too permeable, allowing toxins to escape into the blood, causing a cascade of symptoms.

The Five R's of Gut Healing

When attempting to heal a leaky gut, it's best to go about things in a systematic way. By using a strategic protocol, you can ensure you cover all the bases on your way to good gut health. Functional medicine breaks the process down into the "five R's of gut healing". First, you **remove** foods that cause inflammation to the gut lining. Next, you systematically add back foods and supplements to **replace** digestive enzymes, **reinoculate** your gut with beneficial bacteria, and **repair** the damage with healing foods. Then you can **rebalance** your system with relaxing lifestyle changes.

Remove
ELIMINATE INFLAMMATORY FOODS FROM YOUR DIET

• Begin by removing foods that may be causing inflammation and damage to your gut. This includes certain foods that might trigger allergic reactions, such as grains, soya, eggs, and dairy, or foods that feed undesirable gut flora, such as sugar.

• Minimize exposure to environmental toxins such as smoke, household chemicals, and other pollutants.

• Reduce emotional stress. Yoga, meditation, and deep breathing all help promote a calm state of being.

Replace
ADD BACK ACIDS AND ENZYMES FOR BETTER DIGESTION

• Supplement with hydrochloric acid (HCl) to bolster low stomach acid production.

• Consider supplementing with digestive enzymes (available at health food shops) to aid digestion and help with assimilation of nutrients.

• Use digestive bitters (available at health food shops) to energize and tone your entire digestive system.

Sugars and other carbs contribute to an overgrowth of bad gut flora, so eliminating them is the first step.

Supplements such as digestive enzymes can help your digestive system function better.

Reinoculate

SUPPLEMENT GOOD BACTERIA THROUGH PROBIOTICS

- You can add beneficial bacteria by taking a GAPS-friendly probiotic supplement.

- Eat probiotic foods, such as fermented vegetables, yogurt, and cultured cream.

- Drink probiotic beverages, such as kefir.

Home-made yogurt contains good bacteria that help balance your gut's microbiome.

Repair

FIX GUT DAMAGE WITH SUPPORTIVE FOODS

- Home-made stock and bone broths contain gelatine, which is soothing and helps repair the gut lining.

- Omega-3 fatty acids help reduce inflammation.

- In extreme cases, consult with a certified GAPS practitioner or other qualified medical professional for further supplementation.

Rebalance

MAKE CALMING LIFESTYLE CHANGES

- When you eat, make sure you are in a calm, relaxed state, which makes your digestive system more effective. Eat slowly, put down your fork between bites, and chew your food thoroughly.

- Consider incorporating yoga, meditation, breathing techniques, or similar practices to increase relaxation. Make sure you schedule time to unwind.

- Consider professional help if you're having trouble managing your stress levels and emotional responses.

Home-made stock contains gelatine and fatty acids that help gut repair.

Yoga is one way to relax and calm your system so that it functions better.

Pillars of the Diet

A core selection of healing foods supplies the nutrients your gut needs. Some require special preparation in advance, so that they're ready to eat when you reach the later diet stages and are able to tolerate them.

Healthy Fats

WHAT Lard, tallow, duck or chicken fat, responsibly and sustainably sourced coconut oil and palm oil, and ghee.

WHY Healthy fats are integral to gut healing. Although fats have been demonized for decades, research has started to catch up with the traditional viewpoint of fats as nutrient-dense, health-building foods.

HOW If you've been eating a low-fat diet, you may have difficulty digesting fats because your gallbladder and liver have become lazy at bile production. Start with a small amount, add beetroot to your diet to support the production of bile, and temporarily supplement with ox bile as your body adjusts.

Ghee is a healthy fat you can use for cooking.

Stocks and broths provide healing gelatine to repair intestinal damage.

Stocks and Broths

WHAT Stocks and broths.

WHY Stock and its longer-cooking cousin, bone broth, are exceptionally healing to the gut lining. Gelatine, which comes from the collagen in bones, soothes inflammation and helps the gut repair more quickly. Stocks and broths also are excellent sources of amino acids and protein — and they help stretch your budget too.

HOW Add meaty bones and stock to purified water. An acid, such as cider vinegar or lemon juice, helps bring out the minerals from the bones.

Meat

WHAT Meat, poultry, seafood, and animal fats.

WHY Animal products are incredibly dense in the vitamins and minerals your gut needs to heal properly.

HOW Choose grass-fed, free-range, or wild rather than farmed animal products when possible. Animals are healthiest when they're eating the diet they were designed to eat, and the healthier the animal is, the healthier it will be for you. Always try to buy animal products free of extra hormones, which may interfere with your endocrine system and cause allergic reactions.

Red meats are a diet staple, and provide key vitamins and minerals.

Fermented Vegetables

WHAT Sauerkraut, cultured vegetables, and pickles.

WHY Fermented foods are heavy hitters in the battle to heal your gut. The fermentation process allows beneficial bacteria to multiply, and eating the vegetables transfers the healthy microbes to your digestive tract. Fermentation also boosts vegetables' vitamin and mineral content.

HOW You can ferment with just vegetables, salt, and filtered water, or you can add a starter culture. In the first few stages of the diet, you add the juice from cultured vegetables to soup. In later stages, as your gut heals enough to handle more fibrous foods, you consume the vegetables themselves. For long-term balance, plan on consuming fermented foods with every meal.

Cultured Dairy

WHAT Yogurt, kefir, cultured cream, cultured butter, and crème fraîche.

WHY Cultured dairy is another easy and delicious way to get beneficial probiotics into your gut. Many people who have trouble eating dairy can tolerate cultured dairy.

HOW To make cultured dairy, you need the appropriate starter culture, which you can find at health food shops or online. Once you've produced your first culture, you can use it to start your next batch, making it very affordable. Use raw milk from an established farmer, or look for organic, grass-fed dairy products that have been minimally pasteurized and homogenized.

Cultured dairy such as yogurt adds back beneficial probiotics.

Fermented vegetables such as sauerkraut support beneficial bacteria.

The Healthy Gut Diet

The GAPS diet is a specific protocol that begins with a six-stage introduction diet, before you get to the full diet. In this part, you learn how to prepare for the diet and which foods are allowed at the various stages.

What to Expect

To reverse leaky gut and microbial imbalance (dysbiosis), you go through a healing crisis caused by "die-off", when the pathogenic bacteria start to die and leave your system. This is uncomfortable but normal.

All Over

It's normal to feel tired and feverish as your body works to repair itself. As you progress, you'll be amazed at the energy you feel as your body begins to digest and absorb nutrients more effectively.

Emotional

As your body rebalances, it can be overwhelming to cope with the symptoms of die-off and detoxification. Know where you can get support when you need it, for example by turning to family and friends.

Small Intestine

Cramps and gas are common symptoms of the diet, especially in the early stages. Back off probiotic foods, or consult your food journal to see what new food you recently added.

Skin Issues

The largest organ in your body, your skin is directly involved in detoxification. You might have temporary skin issues as your body rids itself of toxins by every available path.

Large Intestine

Diarrhoea is another die-off symptom. Drink extra water or broth to replace lost fluid. Constipation is also common. If you are prone, start with the full diet for 6 months.

Weight Loss

It's quite likely you'll lose weight on the diet. Many people who lose weight during the earlier stages gain a bit when they go on the full GAPS diet, before normalizing at a healthy weight.

DO	DON'T
✓ Start slowly Spend 1–3 months on the full diet before starting the introduction stage, especially if your diet has been full of processed foods and sugar, and lacking in nutrient-dense whole foods.	**✗ Jump right into the intro** Give yourself at least a month to feel comfortable with making stock, broth, fermented vegetables, and cultured dairy before starting the intro diet. Source ingredients and tools before you begin.
✓ Make time Plan to reduce your personal commitments for the duration of the intro diet. Part of the diet is providing your body with adequate rest so you can heal.	**✗ Start at the wrong time** Right before Christmas, a holiday, a big social event such as a wedding, or a big life change like a new job is not the time to begin the intro stage.
✓ Talk about it Decide how you're going to talk to family and friends about your diet. Often it's helpful to tell them you're on a temporary programme that will help you with your uncomfortable symptoms.	**✗ Go out to eat** Avoid eating out in the early stages. In later stages, check the menu and come up with a plan, or call the restaurant in advance to see how they can accommodate your needs.
✓ Take things slow and easy Most people spend 2–5 days at each stage. You can spend up to 7, after which it's time to move on, unless your digestive symptoms are still severe.	**✗ Force yourself to suffer** If your die-off symptoms are too intense, reduce the amount of probiotic foods or supplements for a few days, and then resume.
✓ Support the detox process Brush your skin 5 minutes a day to stimulate your lymphatic system. Take 30-minute detox baths with a cup of sea salt, baking soda, or cider vinegar in warm bath water.	**✗ Cheat for any reason** Remind yourself of all you have to gain. Remember how uncomfortable your symptoms are.

Preparing Yourself

Ensuring your body and mind are in the right place before starting the healthy gut diet increases your chances of success. Follow this timeline to help get both mind and body in good shape.

3–6 Months Before

- Plan exactly when you want to start, ensuring your calendar is free of travel plans or special events you need to attend.

- Begin making healthier choices, such as cutting down on sugar, grains, and fizzy drinks.

- Eliminate any foods for which you suspect you have an allergy or intolerance.

- Begin using healthy fats for everyday cooking.

- Consider finding a buddy to go through the diet with you. Doing it with someone else is more fun and holds you accountable, which gives you a better chance of sticking with it.

- If you haven't already, read the book **Gut and Psychology Syndrome** by Dr Natasha Campbell-McBride.

1–3 Months Before

- Experiment making one full-diet recipe per week, building up to all full-diet meals and snacks.

- Source any supplements you'll be using on the diet.

- Source any cultures you'll need for dairy products.

- Speak to your doctor about the diet. Find out which supplements and medications you need to continue for the duration of the introduction diet.

- Consider finding a certified GAPS practitioner or online community for support.

- Begin to tell family and friends about your plan, so you can count on their understanding and support.

- Mentally prepare for the diet. List the symptoms you want to stop, and write down how your life will change after you've healed.

2 Weeks Before

- Make sauerkraut and store it in the fridge, so you have fermented vegetable juice for Stages 1 and 2.

- If necessary, order meat and bones from a local butcher or farmer.

- Resist the urge to binge one last time before you start!

1 Week Before

- Plan and shop for your first week of meals.

- Prepare large batches of stock, which you can use to make soup. Freeze some and store some in the fridge.

- If dairy isn't an issue for you, make yogurt or cultured cream for the first week.

Keeping a Food Journal

A food journal can be a powerful tool while you're going through the stages of the GAPS introduction. As you begin to add foods back into your diet, a food journal helps you detect any intolerances. It also helps you track your progress as you heal your leaky gut and make your way towards improved health.

DATE: January 15

Stage 1

Meal	Food	Drink	Digestive Change	Mood Change
Breakfast	Chicken Vegetable Soup	750ml (1¼ pints) water, upon waking	Morning bowel movement	Woke up rested
Snack	Butternut Squash Soup	500ml (16fl oz) water, throughout morning	None	Alert, clear-headed
Lunch	Chicken Vegetable Soup	250ml (8 fl oz) water, 30 minutes before meal	None	None
Snack	Butternut Squash Soup	500ml (16fl oz) water, throughout afternoon	None	Slightly tired before meal (add more fat at lunch?)
Dinner	Lemon Peppercorn Poached Chicken Breast	250ml (8 fl oz) water, 30 minutes before meal	Gas, cramping (possible die-off?)	None
Snack	Butternut Squash Soup	250ml (8 fl oz) water, throughout evening	None	None

Preparing Your Kitchen and Pantry

Having the tools and ingredients you need for the healthy gut diet to hand before you begin makes everything go more smoothly when you start.

Sourcing Ingredients

Before you begin the diet, start to source your ingredients. Look for places to get grass-fed, free-range meats, bones, animal fats, coconut oil, ghee, filtered water, and organic vegetables. For meats, bones, animal fats, and organic vegetables, try your local farmers' market. Check websites like eatwild.com or localharvest.org to find producers who have healthy and sustainable practices. Larger supermarkets, online delivery services, or health food shops are another option. Coconut oil, ghee, and filtered waters are easy to source from health food shops.

Making Ahead

You'll save time and make your life much easier if you cook some food in advance:

- **Stocks and broths** Cook these in advance and store them in the fridge (up to 10 days if there's a solid layer of fat to preserve it) or freezer.

- **Soups** Create soups from the broths and store these for future meals.

- **Ferments and cultures** You need to start these 7 days before you plan to eat them. You'll need fermented juices for the early stages of the diet.

- **Ghee** You can make ghee from your own butter if you prefer not to use shop-bought.

Specialized Tools

In addition to the cooking equipment you usually use – kitchen scales, measuring jugs, knives, baking trays and dishes, heavy-bottomed pans, and so on – you'll find yourself making use of more specialized kitchen equipment on the healthy gut diet:

FINE-MESH SIEVE This helps you strain spices such as peppercorns from cooked sauces in the diet's early stages.

STOCKPOT This is an essential pan for making stocks, broths, and soups.

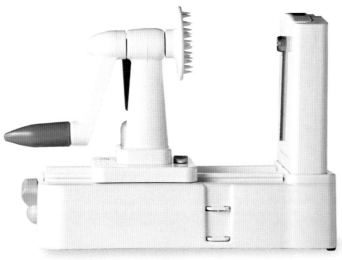

SPIRALIZER This fun tool enables you to make healthy, gluten-free "pasta" from vegetables.

SLOW COOKER This appliance is a handy alternative to making stocks, broths, and soups on the hob.

GLASS JARS You'll used these to store broths and stocks, as well as to hold ferments and cultures.

FLAMEPROOF CASSEROLE For casseroles, one-pot meals, and more.

HAND BLENDER This appliance is handy for puréeing vegetables for smooth soups.

WIDE-MOUTH FUNNEL This is helpful for pouring stocks and cultures into jars for storage.

JUICER This appliance easily extracts juice from fruits and vegetables for making antioxidant-rich drinks.

Planning Ahead

When starting the healthy gut diet, you might feel overwhelmed by the new ingredients and techniques required. But in a few weeks, or even just a few days, these things will become familiar and even routine. In the meantime, developing a plan can help.

Planning Your Meals

- **Keep it simple** Especially in the earliest stages of the intro diet, opt for soup for most meals. Choose two or three for the week, and double the recipes if necessary, so you can freeze individual portions.

- **Cook in advance** In later stages, depending on your family or lifestyle, plan to cook three or four meals a week and save the rest for leftovers.

- **Get creative** Have breakfast for dinner or dinner for breakfast if you like.

Buying Ingredients

- **Stay local** Find a good source of whole chicken and beef bones, preferably free-range and grass-fed. Search online for local farmers or delivery services, or you may be able to get what you need at your local health food shop or farmers' market.

- **Choose quality** If you can't find grass-fed, free-range meats, buy the highest quality you can find and afford. Many people have healed using what they could buy at their local supermarket.

- **Find healthy fats** Locate sources for coconut oil and butter and any other animal fat (such as lard) if possible. Health food shops and farmers' markets are good sources for these too.

Cooking in Advance

- **Think about variety** Alternate soups so you don't get bored. Have one meat-based soup and one vegetable-based soup on hand, so that you can mix things up.

- **Reduce broths** You can reduce broth so that it takes up less space in the freezer. Simply let it boil until you have half or a quarter of the original volume. Make sure you label the container, so you know how much water to add when you come to use it.

- **Stick to a schedule** Fermenting takes time. It's important to stick to a schedule so that you don't find yourself without vegetables or cultured dairy.

Cooking in advance sets you up for success on the diet.

Storing Food

- **Preserve in jars** The easiest way to store broth and soup is in glass preserving jars, available from grocer's or hardware shops. You can use these in the fridge or freezer. (Be sure to leave some space at the top of the jar for the soup to expand if freezing.) Soup will keep for several months in the freezer before it crystallizes.

- **Vacuum seal** If you have a vacuum sealer, you can use it to store soups in the freezer. Follow the manufacturer's instructions for storing liquids. Vacuum-sealed soup keeps for several months.

- **Freeze or refrigerate** Other foods can be stored in the fridge in glass or plastic containers. If the soup has a thick layer of fat on top, it'll keep for up to 10 days.

Broths and soups can be stored in jars in your fridge or freezer.

SAVING MONEY

If you're on a budget, there are plenty of options to consider for saving money on the diet:

- Your local farmers' market is a great source for organic vegetables, meats, and fats. These are often available in smaller quantities than you might have to buy at the supermarket.

- Ask for "seconds" when you shop. These are vegetables that aren't cosmetically perfect but offer the same nutritional value, often at a fraction of the cost.

- Aim to choose vegetables that are in season, when they're less expensive and easier to find.

- Try growing your own vegetables. Even a window box or a few containers can yield a worthwhile harvest.

- For meat and bones, consider buying a half- or quarter-cow from a local farmer, or split the order with a friend. Buying direct and in bulk is a great way to save money.

- Keep in mind that bones are often very inexpensive.

- Making broth and stock-based soups helps you stretch your budget without sacrificing nutritional healing.

Intro Diet

Welcome to the start of your journey! Beginning a diet like this is a big step towards restoring your health. As you get started, be gentle with yourself. Keep things as simple as possible, and give yourself time to rest and heal.

How This Stage Works

- **Elimination** At the beginning, you'll eliminate major irritants, potential allergens, and possible sensitivities that might be contributing to your gut dysbiosis.

- **Microbiome** In Stage 1, bad bacteria have lost their food source – sugar. As a result, they begin to starve and die, and to move out of your body.

- **Timing** Plan to spend 2–5 days at each stage. Some people spend as many as 7 days on a stage, but at that point, you should move on to the next stage unless your digestive symptoms are still severe.

What You Can Expect

- **Die-off** As bad bacteria die, they release toxins. These substances can cause gas, bloating, diarrhoea, and cramping. The worst symptoms usually last only a few days. Be strong, rest as much as you need to, and keep in mind that this stage is only temporary and is the first step towards regaining your health.

- **Adjustments** In Stage 1, you're getting rid of foods you've always eaten. Embrace the idea of new staple foods, new routines, and new mind-sets.

- **Boredom** The foods in Stage 1 are limited on purpose. Keeping things simple can mean you're eating the same meal over and over. Vary things as much as you can while still making things easy on yourself.

Home-made stock is a staple at this stage of the diet.

What You Can Eat

MEAT AND MEAT PRODUCTS These form the basis of this stage. Animal products are an important source of protein and fats, and they're rich in the vitamins and minerals needed for gut healing.

- **Home-made stocks** Sip stocks made from beef, chicken, fish, turkey, or lamb between meals, or use as a base for soups. Commercially bought stock is not the same and cannot be substituted.

- **Boiled meat** Your meat must be well boiled at this stage. Reserve meat, fat, and connective tissue for stock to use in other recipes.

- **Healthy fats** Use good fats such as tallow, lard, chicken, goose, or duck fat for cooking and in soups. Coconut oil also can be used. These fats are rich in the minerals that help heal your gut.

VEGETABLES AND VEGETABLE PRODUCTS You can eat vegetables if they're well cooked; don't eat fermented vegetables at this stage. All types of vegetables are healthy, but to start with, avoid more fibrous vegetables to give your gut a rest.

- **Cooked vegetables** Vegetables must be well cooked and should be peeled. Avoid fibrous vegetables such as cabbage and asparagus, and remove any fibrous parts, such as the stems of cauliflower or broccoli.

- **Juice only** You can use only the juice of fermented vegetables at this stage, because cabbage is too fibrous. Try adding 1 teaspoon to soup, ensuring that the soup has cooled to lukewarm so that the beneficial bacteria aren't destroyed.

TEA

Buy a bunch of fresh mint and some fresh root ginger, or natural, organic loose-leaf chamomile tea. To make the tea, steep 1 tablespoon of ginger and 1 tablespoon of mint, or 1 tablespoon of chamomile tea, in a cup of boiling water for 5–6 minutes. Stir in 1 teaspoon of raw honey, 1 teaspoon of coconut oil, and/or 1 tablespoon of fresh lemon juice to taste, then strain and serve.

CULTURED DAIRY This is allowed at this stage for those who don't have an allergy. Although dairy has received a bad reputation recently, for those who can tolerate it, it's a great source of beneficial probiotics, protein, and fats.

- **Cultured dairy** If you have no allergy to dairy, you can add home-made yogurt, cultured cream, or kefir (which have been cultured no less than 24 hours) at this stage.

- **Home-made dairy** This is the only acceptable type of dairy product during the intro stage. You can experiment with commercial dairy products when you're on the full GAPS diet, but not at this stage.

- **Intolerance** If you suspect dairy intolerance, wait a minimum of 6 months before attempting to reintroduce it.

Yogurt and other cultured dairy products provide helpful probiotics (if you don't have a dairy intolerance).

Beetroot and Beef Short Rib Borscht combines well-cooked vegetables and healing meat.

Meal Plan

STAGE 1

Time in the kitchen is essential for success with from-scratch, gut-healing recipes. Set aside time for planning before starting the diet or moving to the next stage, so you can develop your cooking skills and your shopping list.

NEW STAGE-SPECIFIC CHOICES and recommendations include the following:

- **Probiotic vegetable juice** Begin making a double batch of fermented vegetables at least 7 days before you start the diet. Save the vegetables to incorporate into later stages.

- **Probiotic dairy** If tolerated, begin making a cultured dairy product a few days before starting the diet. Try either Yogurt, Cultured Cream, or Kefir.

- **Home-made stock** Make a double batch of Chicken Stock and a single batch of Meat Stock 2 days before you begin, so it's ready for sipping and for making soups. Plan to make extra to freeze. Add other stocks as your gut health improves.

- **Tea** Chamomile, mint, lemon, raw honey, and/or ginger.

- **Soup** Make two or three soups, plus extra to freeze.

- **Mains** Add one or more main courses for lunch or dinner later in your first week, and eat the leftovers for other meals. Try Beetroot and Beef Short Rib Borscht, Stewed Beef Porridge, or Lemon Peppercorn Poached Chicken Breast.

Sweet-and-Sour Chicken Vegetable Soup is hearty comfort food for any meal.

SUNDAY

BREAKFAST

Chicken Stock
Stage 1, page 59

Juice from Fermented Mixed Vegetables
Stage 1, page 66

Yogurt (optional)
Stage 1, page 74

LUNCH

Chicken Stock
Stage 1, page 59

Juice from Fermented Mixed Vegetables
Stage 1, page 66

Yogurt (optional)
Stage 1, page 74

DINNER

Chicken Stock
Stage 1, page 59

Juice from Fermented Mixed Vegetables
Stage 1, page 66

Yogurt (optional)
Stage 1, page 74

SNACKS

Tea or home-made chicken, beef, or fish stock
Stage 1

ONE-WEEK SAMPLE MEAL PLAN

MONDAY	TUESDAY	WEDNESDAY	THURSDAY	FRIDAY	SATURDAY
Chicken Stock Stage 1, page 59	**Chicken Stock** Stage 1, page 59	**Meat Stock** Stage 1, page 59	**Chicken Stock** Stage 1, page 59	**Meat Stock** Stage 1, page 59	**Chicken Stock** Stage 1, page 59
Juice from Fermented Mixed Vegetables Stage 1, page 66	**Juice from Fermented Mixed Vegetables** Stage 1, page 66	**Juice from Fermented Mixed Vegetables** Stage 1, page 66	**Juice from Fermented Mixed Vegetables** Stage 1, page 66	**Juice from Fermented Mixed Vegetables** Stage 1, page 66	**Juice from Fermented Mixed Vegetables** Stage 1, page 66
Yogurt (optional) Stage 1, page 74	**Yogurt** (optional) Stage 1, page 74	**Yogurt** (optional) Stage 1, page 74	**Yogurt** (optional) Stage 1, page 74	**Yogurt** (optional) Stage 1, page 74	**Yogurt** (optional) Stage 1, page 74
Chicken Stock Stage 1, page 59	**Chicken Stock** Stage 1, page 59	**Classic Chicken Soup** Stage 1, page 84	**Carrot Beetroot Soup** Stage 1, page 86	**Three-Onion Soup** Stage 1, page 93	**Stewed Beef Porridge** Stage 1, page 100
Juice from Fermented Mixed Vegetables Stage 1, page 66	**Juice from Fermented Mixed Vegetables** Stage 1, page 66	**Juice from Fermented Mixed Vegetables** Stage 1, page 66	**Juice from Fermented Mixed Vegetables** Stage 1, page 66	**Juice from Fermented Mixed Vegetables** Stage 1, page 66	**Juice from Fermented Mixed Vegetables** Stage 1, page 66
Yogurt (optional) Stage 1, page 74	**Yogurt** (optional) Stage 1, page 74	**Yogurt** (optional) Stage 1, page 74	**Yogurt** (optional) Stage 1, page 74	**Yogurt** (optional) Stage 1, page 74	**Yogurt** (optional) Stage 1, page 74
Chicken Stock Stage 1, page 59	**Classic Chicken Soup** Stage 1, page 84	**Carrot Beetroot Soup** Stage 1, page 86	**Three-Onion Soup** Stage 1, page 93	**Stewed Beef Porridge** Stage 1, page 100	**Lemon Peppercorn Poached Chicken Breast** Stage 1, page 101
Juice from Fermented Mixed Vegetables Stage 1, page 66	**Juice from Fermented Mixed Vegetables** Stage 1, page 66	**Juice from Fermented Mixed Vegetables** Stage 1, page 66	**Juice from Fermented Mixed Vegetables** Stage 1, page 66	**Juice from Fermented Mixed Vegetables** Stage 1, page 66	**Juice from Fermented Mixed Vegetables** Stage 1, page 66
Yogurt (optional) Stage 1, page 74	**Yogurt** (optional) Stage 1, page 74	**Yogurt** (optional) Stage 1, page 74	**Yogurt** (optional) Stage 1, page 74	**Yogurt** (optional) Stage 1, page 74	**Yogurt** (optional) Stage 1, page 74
Tea or home-made chicken, beef, or fish stock Stage 1	**Tea or home-made chicken, beef, or fish stock** Stage 1	**Tea or home-made chicken, beef, or fish stock** Stage 1	**Tea or home-made chicken, beef, or fish stock** Stage 1	**Tea or home-made chicken, beef, or fish stock** Stage 1	**Tea or home-made chicken, beef, or fish stock** Stage 1

STAGE 2 Intro Diet

Stage 2 continues in much the same way as Stage 1, with one big addition: eggs. Begin adding a raw egg yolk to a portion of soup, and increase until you're having two or three yolks with every portion of soup.

How This Stage Works

- **Some new, some old** Continue eating Stage 1 foods while you add new Stage 2 foods. You can still keep things simple and easy as you add some variety to your diet.

- **Slow progress** If you suspect an egg allergy might be to blame for any of your digestive issues, omit eggs for a day, see how you feel, and then try again. Use the same procedure for all new foods as you slowly add them to your diet.

- **Some relief** Keep going with the diet, and realize that even though there may be relief from some of your symptoms, you aren't yet fully healed.

What You Can Expect

- **Die-off** Die-off should have slowed down or stopped by now, although you might still experience it in patches. Symptoms of die-off and allergy or intolerance to foods often look the same, so consult your food journal as you add new foods to determine which is at play.

- **A healthy routine** Hopefully you've settled into a groove with the diet by now. Stick to making stocks and soups, now adding stews.

- **Some improvement** You should be experiencing less gas, bloating, and discomfort, although this does depend on where you started in terms of symptoms.

Chicken Vegetable Ratatouille is a gut-healing version of the traditional French comfort dish.

What You Can Eat

STOCKS, SOUPS, AND STEWS These form the basis of Stage 2 and are an easy and satisfying way to stay fuelled. They also make your life simpler because you're packing lots of gut-healing nutrients into an easy-to-heat-and-eat package.

- **Stocks and soups** Continue with stocks and soups, enjoying your favourites from Stage 1.

- **Stews** You can increase stews that have more meat and vegetables and less stock.

- **Boiled meats** Continue with meats that have been well boiled in soups, stews, or casseroles.

BOILED VEGETABLES AND FERMENTED JUICES

These are the best ways to enjoy vegetables at this stage. Boiling vegetables makes them easier to digest. It does remove some of the nutrients, so it's best to consume the water they were boiled in, as with soup.

- **Boiled vegetables** Peeled, nonfibrous vegetables such as carrots, onions, beetroot, green beans, and broccoli (remove the stalks) that have been well boiled are easiest to tolerate.

- **Fermented vegetable juice** This continues to work well added to soups. Increase the amount, adjusting if the die-off reaction gets too intense.

SEASONING AND SPICES

For seasoning, use sea salt and peppercorns, removing the peppercorns before eating the finished dish. You also can use fresh herbs now. Rosemary, basil, tarragon, and sage are classic herbs for soups. Tie them with kitchen twine to make them easy to remove.

FATS AND DAIRY If tolerated, these are great sources of protein and nutrients for your diet. Many people who can't tolerate pasteurized and homogenized dairy can tolerate raw dairy, which allows them to enjoy the nutritional value without the digestive symptoms.

- **Animal fats and coconut oil** These healthy fats continue to be good additions.

- **Ghee** Ghee can be added at this stage. Begin with 1 teaspoon per day and gradually increase, watching out for any intolerance.

- **Cod liver oil** This is another allowable addition at this stage. It's not used for cooking, but should be taken by the spoonful or in capsules. Check the GAPS website for recommendations.

- **Dairy products** If you can tolerate them, continue with dairy products. You can increase quantities at this stage.

Ghee is an essential fat you will use from this stage onwards.

Meal Plan

By now, you've probably started to get a handle on the ingredients and quantities you need to stock, how to prepare vegetables in bulk, and ways to store what you've produced. Stage 2 continues with much of the same, so keep building on your successes from Stage 1 while adding some new choices.

NEW STAGE-SPECIFIC CHOICES and recommendations include the following:

- **Probiotic vegetable juice** Try adding a fermentation you didn't make in Stage 1, because the juice is still essential.

- **Dairy** Start with Home-Churned Butter, and use it to make high-quality fat Ghee.

- **Home-made stocks** Continue with stocks you're already using, and add a batch or two of a new one. Choices include chicken, turkey, fish, beef, or lamb.

- **Soups** Try Egg Drop Soup and Vegetable Beef Stewp. Add fresh egg yolks to all your soups and stews for extra healing.

- **Mains** New choices include Braised Beef (or Turkey) Burgers, Asian Braised Turkey Meatballs, Chicken-Stuffed Cabbage Rolls, Chicken Vegetable Ratatouille, Chicken Enchilada Casserole, Lemon Rosemary Salmon, and Braised Tomato Sage Turkey Legs.

Braised Beef Burgers are a hearty way to enjoy meat with flavourful cooked vegetables.

	SUNDAY
BREAKFAST	**Chicken Stock** Stage 1, page 59
	Juice from Fermented Mixed Vegetables Stage 1, page 66
	Yogurt (optional) Stage 1, page 74
LUNCH	**Butternut Squash Soup** Stage 1, page 85
	Juice from Fermented Mixed Vegetables Stage 1, page 66
	Yogurt (optional) Stage 1, page 74
DINNER	**Braised Beef Burgers** Stage 2, page 108
	Juice from Fermented Mixed Vegetables Stage 1, page 66
	Yogurt (optional) Stage 1, page 74
SNACKS	**Tea or home-made chicken, beef, or fish stock** Stage 1

ONE-WEEK SAMPLE MEAL PLAN

MONDAY	TUESDAY	WEDNESDAY	THURSDAY	FRIDAY	SATURDAY
Meat Stock Stage 1, page 58	**Chicken Stock** Stage 1, page 59	**Meat Stock** Stage 1, page 58	**Chicken Stock** Stage 1, page 59	**Meat Stock** Stage 1, page 58	**Chicken Stock** Stage 1, page 59
Juice from Fermented Mixed Vegetables Stage 1, page 66	**Juice from Fermented Mixed Vegetables** Stage 1, page 66	**Juice from Fermented Mixed Vegetables** Stage 1, page 66	**Juice from Fermented Mixed Vegetables** Stage 1, page 66	**Juice from Fermented Mixed Vegetables** Stage 1, page 66	**Juice from Fermented Mixed Vegetables** Stage 1, page 66
Yogurt (optional) Stage 1, page 74	**Yogurt** (optional) Stage 1, page 74	**Yogurt** (optional) Stage 1, page 74	**Yogurt** (optional) Stage 1, page 74	**Yogurt** (optional) Stage 1, page 74	**Yogurt** (optional) Stage 1, page 74
Egg Drop Soup Stage 2, page 106	**Braised Beef Burgers** Stage 2, page 108	**Egg Drop Soup** Stage 2, page 106	**Creamy Tomato Soup** Stage 1, page 96	**Asian Braised Turkey Meatballs** Stage 2, page 110	**Lemon Rosemary Salmon** Stage 2, page 115
Juice from Fermented Mixed Vegetables Stage 1, page 66	**Juice from Fermented Mixed Vegetables** Stage 1, page 66	**Juice from Fermented Mixed Vegetables** Stage 1, page 66	**Juice from Fermented Mixed Vegetables** Stage 1, page 66	**Juice from Fermented Mixed Vegetables** Stage 1, page 66	**Juice from Fermented Mixed Vegetables** Stage 1, page 66
Yogurt (optional) Stage 1, page 74	**Yogurt** (optional) Stage 1, page 74	**Yogurt** (optional) Stage 1, page 74	**Yogurt** (optional) Stage 1, page 74	**Yogurt** (optional) Stage 1, page 74	**Yogurt** (optional) Stage 1, page 74
Chicken Vegetable Ratatouille Stage 2, page 112	**Butternut Squash Soup** Stage 1, page 85	**Chicken Vegetable Ratatouille** Stage 2, page 112	**Asian Braised Turkey Meatballs** Stage 2, page 110	**Lemon Rosemary Salmon** Stage 2, page 115	**Creamy Tomato Soup** Stage 1, page 96
Juice from Fermented Mixed Vegetables Stage 1, page 66	**Juice from Fermented Mixed Vegetables** Stage 1, page 66	**Juice from Fermented Mixed Vegetables** Stage 1, page 66	**Juice from Fermented Mixed Vegetables** Stage 1, page 66	**Juice from Fermented Mixed Vegetables** Stage 1, page 66	**Juice from Fermented Mixed Vegetables** Stage 1, page 66
Yogurt (optional) Stage 1, page 74	**Yogurt** (optional) Stage 1, page 74	**Yogurt** (optional) Stage 1, page 74	**Yogurt** (optional) Stage 1, page 74	**Yogurt** (optional) Stage 1, page 74	**Yogurt** (optional) Stage 1, page 74
Tea or home-made chicken, beef, or fish stock Stage 1	**Tea or home-made chicken, beef, or fish stock** Stage 1	**Tea or home-made chicken, beef, or fish stock** Stage 1	**Tea or home-made chicken, beef, or fish stock** Stage 1	**Tea or home-made chicken, beef, or fish stock** Stage 1	**Tea or home-made chicken, beef, or fish stock** Stage 1

Intro Diet

If, for the sake of convenience, you've been eating mostly soups for Stages 1 and 2, Stage 3 might feel like a revelation. Scrambled eggs for breakfast? Squash pancakes? Nut butter? It's a whole new world!

How This Stage Works

- **Gut calming** In Stage 3, you're building on the progress you've made in calming your gut and removing reactive foods from your diet.

- **More good bacteria** You're continuing to make headway in controlling your gut's population of challenging bacteria, introducing more beneficial bacteria, and creating a more favourable environment for the bacteria to thrive.

- **New foods** You'll test the waters with new foods and become more deliberate about the inhabitants of your microbiome.

What You Can Expect

- **Less digestive distress** By now, your digestive distress has probably calmed down quite a bit. Moving forward, any recurrence of symptoms is likely to be die-off, especially as you add in probiotic foods.

- **Trial and error** If you experience recurring digestive symptoms, you can step back to the preceding stage for a day and then move forward again. Alternatively, check your food diary to see what food you recently added, remove it, and see how your body responds.

- **Sensitivity testing** You can now test a suspected food for sensitivity. If you don't show any sensitivity, try reintroducing the food in a few weeks or even months. As your gut heals, you might be able to tolerate foods you never thought you'd be able to eat again.

> **SUPPLEMENTS**
> During Stage 3, you'll want to add a GAPS-legal therapeutic probiotic supplement. (For specific recommendations, consult the GAPS website.) But start slowly! Begin with a small dose – such as half a capsule – and gradually increase until you're taking the full dose.

Sweet-and-Sour Red Slaw is a tasty way to enjoy fermented vegetables.

What You Can Eat

EGGS Cooked eggs in all their marvellous forms are a focus in this stage, providing protein and new textures. As well as being delicious, soft- and hard-boiled eggs make a convenient, portable snack.

- **Quality** Remember to choose the highest-quality eggs possible.

- **Quantity** Plan to buy more than a dozen — you might find yourself eating eggs for breakfast, lunch, and dinner.

- **Cooking** Cook your eggs more gently at first, for example soft-boiled rather than hard-boiled. Use plenty of animal fat, coconut oil, or ghee when scrambling eggs.

Asparagus Fried Eggs is a delicious recipe for adding cooked eggs and vegetables to your diet.

FERMENTED VEGETABLES You can now eat the vegetables instead of just the juice. There are two key words to remember as you begin: *start slowly*.

- **Start small** Try 1 or 2 teaspoons with a meal, and see how your body responds. If your digestive symptoms recur with fermented vegetables, die-off is the likely culprit. Don't panic, and definitely don't lose hope. As uncomfortable as it can be, die-off is a good sign. You're making progress!

- **Small amounts** Reduce the amount of vegetables you're eating, even if that means you're only eating $1/2$ teaspoon of vegetables at a time.

- **Spread them out** You can also reduce the frequency, perhaps eating them with only one meal instead of all three.

- **Reduce symptoms** Do what you need to do to reduce your symptoms to a level you can live with. As your symptoms abate, increase the amount and frequency of vegetables until you're eating 1 or 2 tablespoons with each meal, listening to your body's responses carefully to set the pace.

HEALTHY FATS AND MORE In Stage 3, you will also add avocado and nut butter. Mash avocado to make simple guacamole, and eat nut butters on squash pancakes or simply off a spoon.

- **Start with almond butter** As always, go slowly and see how your body reacts. If you find that you react to one type of nut butter, try another.

- **Move beyond boiled vegetables** You can now add fully cooked (not just boiled) vegetables.

  - **Keep up the broth** Continue eating foods you enjoy from Stages 1 and 2. Sipping broth in the morning or between meals is still nourishing and healing for your gut.

Meal Plan

STAGE 3

You've made it to the halfway point in the introduction diet. More options now can mean more stress if you let it. Remember, you don't have to use every recipe available to you. It's fine to keep things simple. But bear in mind that including new recipes as you move forwards helps you increase variety and better nourish your gut and body.

NEW STAGE-SPECIFIC CHOICES and recommendations include the following:

- **Probiotic vegetables** Red Cabbage Kraut and Sweet-and-Sour Red Slaw are two tasty ways to get your ferments.

- **Dairy** Continue including in your diet probiotic and cultured dairy, as tolerated.

- **Hard-boiled eggs** This new addition is a satisfying, high-protein snack or meal.

- **Mains** Try Sauerkraut Scramble, Santa Fe Breakfast Tostadas, Asparagus Fried Eggs, Roasted Butternut Squash Pancakes, Easy Avocado Omelette, and Aromatic Chicken with Mushrooms.

Simple Roasted Root Vegetables are great as a side with Aromatic Chicken with Mushrooms, or on their own.

SUNDAY

BREAKFAST

Easy Avocado Omelette
Stage 3, page 125

Fermented Mixed Vegetables
Stage 1, page 66

LUNCH

Chicken Vegetable Soup
Stage 1, page 88

DINNER

Roasted Butternut Squash Pancakes
Stage 3, page 124

Hard-boiled eggs
Stage 3

SNACKS

Tea or home-made stock
Stage 1

ONE-WEEK SAMPLE MEAL PLAN

MONDAY	TUESDAY	WEDNESDAY	THURSDAY	FRIDAY	SATURDAY
Sauerkraut Scramble Stage 3, page 120	**Asparagus Fried Eggs** Stage 3, page 122 **Red Cabbage Kraut** Stage 3, page 64	**Easy Avocado Omelette** Stage 3, page 125 **Fermented Mixed Vegetables** Stage 1, page 66	**Sauerkraut Scramble** Stage 3, page 120	**Asparagus Fried Eggs** Stage 3, page 122 **Red Cabbage Kraut** Stage 3, page 64	**Santa Fe Breakfast Tostadas** Stage 3, page 121 **Fermented Mixed Vegetables** Stage 1, page 66
Roasted Butternut Squash Pancakes Stage 3, page 124 **Hard-boiled eggs** Stage 3	**Garlicky Greens Soup** Stage 1, page 89	**Aromatic Chicken with Mushrooms** Stage 3, page 126	**Egg Drop Soup** Stage 2, page 106	**Braised Beef Burgers** Stage 2, page 108	**Egg Drop Soup** Stage 2, page 106
Chicken Vegetable Soup Stage 1, page 88	**Aromatic Chicken with Mushrooms** Stage 3, page 126	**Garlicky Greens Soup** Stage 1, page 89	**Braised Beef Burgers** Stage 2, page 108	**Egg Drop Soup** Stage 2, page 106	**Lemon Rosemary Salmon** Stage 2, page 115
Tea or home-made stock Stage 1	**Tea or home-made stock** Stage 1	**Tea or home-made stock** Stage 1	**Tea or home-made stock** Stage 1	**Tea or home-made stock** Stage 1	**Tea or home-made stock** Stage 1

STAGE 4 Intro Diet

In Stage 4, you'll start to feel like a normal person again, someone who can eat (mostly) normal food. The addition of baked and roast meats, and breads made from nut and seed flours brings a welcome variety.

How This Stage Works

- **New foods** You can enjoy new foods in Stage 4. Add them in slowly, paying attention to how your body reacts. Just because it's time to add a food to the diet doesn't mean the food is right for you. Your body will let you know. Gas, bloating, or diarrhoea means you're not yet ready for that food.

- **Juice inclusion** At this stage, you can add some simple vegetable juices. Although beneficial, juicing is not strictly necessary, so if it's too much for you right now, set it aside and add it later.

- **Maintain** It's easy to feel like you've healed at this stage and can go back to your former habits. Don't!

What You Can Expect

- **Fewer symptoms** Most likely, your symptoms will have calmed down completely by now. You should be experiencing increased energy and vitality.

- **More variety** Bread made with nut or seed flour gives you more options for meals during Stage 4.

- **Eating out** Although eating out is easier now, call ahead or check the restaurant's menu online to make sure you'll be able to avoid prohibited ingredients, especially oils. Decide on menu options that will work for you before you get there.

Properly soaked and dried seeds, if you can tolerate them, are back on the menu. Or try seed flours for lots of new baking options.

Everyday Grain-Free Bread made with nut flours is a welcome addition.

What You Can Eat

MEATS You get more options for preparing meat at this stage of the diet. You can always stick to your favourites from earlier stages, but more variety is now available.

- **More choices** Beef, chicken, lamb, and fish are all good options, depending on your tastes.

- **Baking and roasting** These meat preparation methods are now allowed, adding more flavour and texture to the finished dishes.

- **Barbecuing and frying** Avoid these preparation methods. They're still not allowed.

VEGETABLE JUICE At this stage of the diet, you can incorporate juice. This also gives you a way to promote detox. You can enjoy vegetable juices as a drink, but you'll need to work up to it.

- **Carrot juice** Begin slowly, with 1 teaspoon of carrot juice per day on an empty stomach.

- **Celery, lettuce, and mint juices** Add these to your juicing plan slowly. Find a combination you enjoy.

- **Don't go overboard** Only drink a few tablespoons of juice at a time.

Vegetable juices return to your diet, but need to be introduced slowly.

> ### SUPPLEMENTS
> Continue with your GAPS-approved probiotic. You might also need hydrochloric acid if your body doesn't produce enough and you have heartburn and acid indigestion. Take 1 betaine HCl tablet mid-meal, and increase by 1 tablet at each meal until you feel a warming sensation after taking the pills. Thereafter, take 1 fewer pill mid-meal as your dose, and monitor your reaction. Your dose might get lower as your health improves.

FATS Healthy fats are still a vital part of the diet, and now you get a popular new favourite to add back into your diet. But don't abandon the animal fats. They should be a permanent part of your diet.

- **Cold-pressed olive oil** You can use this fat now. Start sparingly and build up, keeping an eye out for reactions.

- **Animal fats** Continue to use these for sautéing and in soups.

- **Rapeseed, sunflower, and other vegetable oils** These are not permitted.

NUT FLOURS These bring a wealth of new choices. Now you can have gluten-free bread made with nut flours. Suddenly, sandwiches are back on the table, as are gluten-free muffins and empanadas.

- **Nut flour** You can use nut flours to make breads. Seed flour is also acceptable but probably best saved for later stages.

- **Almond flour** Start with almond flour, noticing how your body reacts. Progress slowly with other nut and seed flours. Nuts are often difficult to digest, so pay attention to what your body tells you.

- **Cashew or walnut flour** These are good choices for your next flour.

STAGE 4 Meal Plan

You're now hitting your stride! Having the options of roasting, baking, and grilling gives you a wider range of meat preparation techniques and flavours. Continue to keep things simple, but add variety when you can.

NEW STAGE-SPECIFIC CHOICES and recommendations include the following:

- **Probiotic vegetables** For increased variety, add the probiotic-rich Cultured Spring Vegetables, Cultured Root Vegetables, and Cultured Rainbow Vegetables ferments.

- **Dairy** Continue as tolerated.

- **Mains** Use new ingredients and methods to create recipes you'll love, including Garlic Chicken with Vegetables, Grilled Salmon with Walnut Pesto, "Spaghetti" with Pomodoro Sauce, Oven-Roasted Turkey Meatloaf, Classic Pot Roast with Onions, Minced Beef Stroganoff, and Minced Beef Empanadas.

- **Snacks** Stocks and tea are still available as snacks, but adding some more options will give you variety. Make a double batch of Ginger Pumpkin Muffins or Chicken Muffins and freeze some for later. Or prepare extra vegetables in advance for Green Goddess Juice, Liver-Loving Juice, or Peppery Pear Juice. Crackling Nuts and Crackling Seeds offer a satisfying crunch.

Flavourful sauces combine with "spaghetti" made from courgettes for tasty grain-free meals.

SUNDAY

BREAKFAST

Carrot juice
Stage 4

Easy
Avocado Omelette
Stage 3, page 125

LUNCH

Carrot Beetroot
Soup
Stage 1, page 86

DINNER

Classic Pot Roast
with Onions
Stage 4, page 139

SNACKS

Home-made beef
or chicken stock
Stage 1

Tea
Stage 1

Crackling Nuts
Stage 4, page 143

ONE-WEEK SAMPLE MEAL PLAN

MONDAY	TUESDAY	WEDNESDAY	THURSDAY	FRIDAY	SATURDAY
Carrot juice Stage 4 **Roasted Butternut Squash Pancakes** Stage 3, page 124	**Carrot juice** Stage 4 **Sauerkraut Scramble** Stage 3, page 120	**Carrot juice** Stage 4 **Roasted Butternut Squash Pancakes** Stage 3, page 124	**Carrot or vegetable juice** Stage 4 **Chicken Muffins** Stage 4, page 131	**Liver-Loving Juice** Stage 4, page 133 **Roasted Butternut Squash Pancakes** Stage 3, page 124	**Liver-Loving Juice** Stage 4, page 133 **Chicken Muffins** Stage 4, page 131
Classic Pot Roast with Onions Stage 4, page 139	**Carrot Beetroot Soup** Stage 1, page 86	**Vegetable Beef Stewp** Stage 2, page 107	**"Spaghetti" with Pomodoro Sauce** Stage 4, page 136	**Minced Beef Empanadas** Stage 4, page 142	**Oven-Roasted Turkey Meatloaf** Stage 4, page 138
Vegetable Beef Stewp Stage 2, page 107	**"Spaghetti" with Pomodoro Sauce** Stage 4, page 136	**Minced Beef Empanadas** Stage 4, page 142	**Oven-Roasted Turkey Meatloaf** Stage 4, page 138	**Asparagus Fried Eggs** Stage 3, page 122	**Aromatic Chicken with Mushrooms** Stage 3, page 126 **Simple Roasted Root Vegetables** Stage 3, page 127
Home-made beef or chicken stock Stage 1 **Tea** Stage 1 **Crackling Nuts** Stage 4, page 143	**Home-made beef or chicken stock** Stage 1 **Tea** Stage 1 **Crackling Nuts** Stage 4, page 143	**Home-made beef or chicken stock** Stage 1 **Tea** Stage 1 **Crackling Nuts** Stage 4, page 143	**Home-made beef or chicken stock** Stage 1 **Tea** Stage 1 **Crackling Nuts** Stage 4, page 143	**Home-made beef or chicken stock** Stage 1 **Tea** Stage 1 **Crackling Nuts** Stage 4, page 143	**Home-made beef or chicken stock** Stage 1 **Tea** Stage 1 **Crackling Nuts** Stage 4, page 143

STAGE 5 Intro Diet

With the introduction of raw vegetables and spices in Stage 5, you'll feel like your diet, and your life, is getting back to normal. Fruit also makes a limited appearance now, and after going so long with so little flavour, you'll find it tastes amazingly sweet.

How This Stage Works

- **Some old, some new** Continue with the foods you enjoy from previous stages. You don't have to abandon these recipes, just because you've moved on. Keep on enjoying your core favourites.

- **Increased juicing** Expand the foods you juice to include fruit as well as vegetables. Always aim for a higher percentage of vegetable juice.

- **Dish diversity** Experiment with new recipes, and enjoy the variety of dishes you can prepare and eat now. Also enjoy the fresh flavours of fruit and vegetables again.

What You Can Expect

- **Progress slowly** It can be easy at these later stages to want to race ahead. But when adding new foods, do it slowly. Going too quickly could cause a setback.

- **Watch your reactions** Healing a leaky gut doesn't mean you can tolerate every food. If your body reacts negatively to an added food, eliminate that food. Listen to your body.

- **Enjoy your progress** You'll have more energy now, and are likely to be happy with what you see in the mirror and on the scales. Celebrate your success!

SPICES AND SEASONING

Some dried spices are allowed now. Start with peppercorns, basil, sage, thyme, parsley, ginger, cumin, coriander, paprika, and cloves. You will add more spices in Stage 6 and on the full GAPS diet.

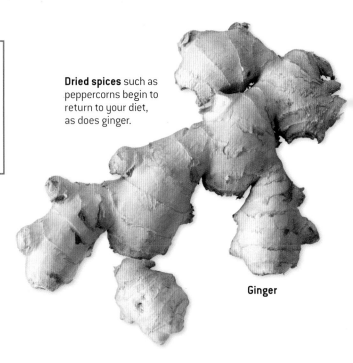

Dried spices such as peppercorns begin to return to your diet, as does ginger.

Ginger

Pink peppercorns

What You Can Eat

RAW VEGETABLES These can now be incorporated into your diet. You'll enjoy their crisp freshness and bright flavours. And having worked your way up to raw vegetables, the door is now open for salads.

- **Bring on the salad** Raw vegetables are now allowed. Salads of all types, flavours, and colours are a welcome change.

- **Start slowly** As always, start gently – with soft lettuce and peeled cucumber.

- **Progress gradually** If you tolerate soft lettuce and peeled cucumber, progress to carrot, tomato, onion, and even cabbage, checking your body's responses.

FRUIT JUICES Fresh fruit juice is back on your menu, as are apples. The latter's delicious, juicy flesh adds natural sweetness to your meals.

- **Fruit juice** In addition to vegetable juice, you can also juice some fruits. Make sure you're keeping track of juices in your food journal, so you can detect any possible sensitivities.

- **Apple, mango, and pineapple juices** You can mix these juices with your vegetable juice. Make the fruit component no more than 20–25 per cent of the mixture. No citrus fruits (other than lemon water) are allowed at this stage.

- **Baked apples** These are a delicious choice for dessert. Try them with cloves for a warming autumn flavour.

Baked apples make a tasty dessert or snack.

Simple salads taste great after you've not eaten fresh greens for a while.

STAGE 5 Meal Plan

Stage 5 presents new ingredient opportunities. Fruits broaden your menu and bring naturally sweet treats and more juices. Raw vegetables offer options for salads and other easily prepared cold dishes that give you a break from cooking.

NEW STAGE-SPECIFIC CHOICES and recommendations include the following:

- **Probiotic vegetables** Keep your ferments going! By Stage 5, you've most likely hit your stride with quantities and timing.

- **Dairy** Continue as tolerated.

- **Mains** Incorporate new choices as you feel able, to keep things interesting and varied. When you can, cook in advance. Try Simple House Salad, Grain-Free Tabbouleh, Easy Chicken Stir-Fry, and Tex-Mex Pulled Pork Burritos.

- **Snacks** Snacks are important because they nourish you between meals and prevent hunger. Try easy-to-make Mini Butternut Squash Soufflés or Guacamole.

Tex-Mex Pulled Pork Burritos served on Almond Flour Wraps are zesty and healing.

SUNDAY

BREAKFAST

Liver-Loving Juice
Stage 4, page 133

Asparagus Fried Eggs
Stage 3, page 122

LUNCH

Grain-Free Tabbouleh
Stage 5, page 147

Pumpkin Bisque
Stage 1, page 94

DINNER

Grilled Salmon with Walnut Pesto
Stage 4, page 135

SNACKS

Liver-Loving Juice
Stage 4, page 133

Apple Pie Stewed Apples
Stage 5, page 154

Tea or home-made stock
Stage 1

ONE-WEEK SAMPLE MEAL PLAN

MONDAY	TUESDAY	WEDNESDAY	THURSDAY	FRIDAY	SATURDAY
Vegetable juice Stage 1 **Easy Avocado Omelette** Stage 3, page 125	**Liver-Loving Juice** Stage 4, page 133 **Sauerkraut Scramble** Stage 3, page 120	**Liver-Loving Juice** Stage 4, page 133 **Asparagus Fried Eggs** Stage 3, page 122	**Green Goddess Juice** Stage 4, page 132 **Easy Avocado Omelette** Stage 3, page 125	**Liver-Loving Juice** Stage 4, page 133 **Sauerkraut Scramble** Stage 3, page 120	**Vegetable juice** Stage 1 **Santa Fe Breakfast Tostadas** Stage 3, page 121
Simple House Salad Stage 5, page 146 **Chicken Vegetable Soup** Stage 1, page 88	**Grain-Free Tabbouleh** Stage 5, page 147 **Pumpkin Bisque** Stage 1, page 94	**Simple House Salad** Stage 5, page 146 **Chicken Vegetable Soup** Stage 1, page 88	**Tex-Mex Pulled Pork Burritos with Almond Flour Wraps** Stage 5, page 152	**Asian Braised Turkey Meatballs** Stage 2, page 110	**Chicken Vegetable Ratatouille** Stage 2, page 112
Easy Chicken Stir-Fry Stage 5, page 151	**Lemon Peppercorn Poached Chicken Breast** Stage 1, page 101	**Tex-Mex Pulled Pork Burritos with Almond Flour Wraps** Stage 5, page 152	**Asian Braised Turkey Meatballs** Stage 2, page 110	**Chicken Vegetable Ratatouille** Stage 2, page 112	**Easy Chicken Stir-Fry** Stage 5, page 151
Green Goddess Juice Stage 4, page 132 **Chicken Muffins** Stage 4, page 131 **Tea or home-made stock** Stage 1	**Peppery Pear Juice** Stage 4, page 132 **Crackling Nuts** Stage 4, page 143 **Tea or home-made stock** Stage 1	**Liver-Loving Juice** Stage 4, page 133 **Baked Cinnamon Walnut Apples** Stage 5, page 155 **Tea or home-made stock** Stage 1	**Green Goddess Juice** Stage 4, page 132 **Guacamole** Stage 5, page 150 **Tea or home-made stock** Stage 1	**Peppery Pear Juice** Stage 4, page 132 **Mini Butternut Squash Soufflés** Stage 5, page 148 **Tea or home-made stock** Stage 1	**Liver-Loving Juice** Stage 4, page 133 **Hard-boiled eggs** Stage 3 **Tea or home-made stock** Stage 1

(STAGE 6) Intro Diet

Congratulate yourself for all the hard work you've put in! As you complete this last stage of the introduction diet, you should reflect on where you started and how far you've come.

How This Stage Works

- **Increased honey and fruit** As you begin to add more honey and fruit, pay careful attention to how your body responds. The amount of honey and fruit that can be tolerated without disrupting blood sugar or gaining weight differs from person to person.

- **More nut consumption** Nuts aren't always easy to digest, even for a healthy gut. As you add more, especially in breads, muffins, and other baked goods, keep a close eye on any increase in your symptoms, and remove the foods that cause trouble.

- **Moderation** This is an important rule to observe moving forward. If a new food works for you, don't go overboard. Bingeing is not healthy behaviour and doesn't contribute to gut health.

What You Can Expect

- **More sweets** As long as honey is the sweetener, you can have more sweets now. Carefully monitor how your body responds, though. If your digestive symptoms return, or if you find yourself getting blood sugar swings, back off the sweets.

- **Weight loss** Some weight loss is normal on the GAPS diet. If you're concerned you've lost too much, wait to see what happens when you go onto the full GAPS diet. Most people find a new, healthy normal once they've been on the full diet.

- **Sense of accomplishment** This is totally appropriate. You've shown great patience and restraint. Great job!

Strawberries

Banana

Honey is the only GAPS-legal sweetener.

What You Can Eat

RAW FRUITS Finally, you should be able to tolerate raw fruit now. Add fruit back into your diet slowly and carefully, starting with these.

- **Raw fruit** Slowly add more raw fruit from the list of GAPS-approved foods.

- **Berries** With their high fibre content, berries are a great place to start.

- **Tinned or preserved fruits** Jams and jellies are not allowed. Stick to whole or chopped fruits with lower sugar.

SWEETENED FOODS With honey as the sweetener, these treats can make a return to your diet. Still, be cautious as you slowly reintroduce these foods. After so long without them, they now might taste too sweet.

- **Experiment with more honey** If you do well with it, you can increase your honey intake. Watch for any carbohydrate sensitivity, such as mood and energy swings, weight gain, or binge behaviour.

- **Desserts** These can be increased during Stage 6. Again, keep an eye out for any sensitivity.

- **Taste changes** Your taste buds are likely to have recalibrated, so you can taste the complex sweetness of dishes.

NUTS Brazil nuts can be added at this stage. As with other foods you reintroduce, be aware of any digestive symptoms you experience and back off as necessary.

Fresh fruit is a healthy way to add some sweetness to your diet. Berries especially are rich in fibre and antioxidants.

Raspberries

Blueberries

Seasonal Mixed-Berry Crostata combines luscious seasonal fruits with a gluten-free crust.

(STAGE 6) Meal Plan

You've made it to Stage 6 of the intro diet. You're more confident in the kitchen and making only small tweaks to your overall plan. Now, a few new ingredients and tasty recipes help keep you healthy and enthusiastic as you head towards the full diet.

NEW STAGE-SPECIFIC CHOICES and recommendations include the following:

- **Probiotic vegetables** Keep your ferments going, and look for your own recipe variations.

- **Dairy** Continue as tolerated.

- **Mains** New options let you tailor your plan to your family's preferences. Try Roasted Brussels Sprout Apple Salad, Scallops Piccata, and Chicken Thigh Puttanesca.

- **Desserts** High-quality home-made desserts are a satisfying and appropriate part of gut health. Try Dairy-Free Key Lime Mousse, Seasonal Mixed-Berry Crostada, Honey Bombs, and Gingered Vanilla Honey Drops.

- **Snacks** Extra snack recipes keep you satisfied throughout the day. Try the Anytime Smoothie or the Olive Raisin Tapenade, which is great as a dip or a topping for roasted meat.

Scallops Piccata is a tasty new addition at this stage, featuring shellfish and home-made butter.

SUNDAY

BREAKFAST

Peppery Pear Juice
Stage 4, page 132

Easy Avocado Omelette
Stage 3, page 125

LUNCH

Simple House Salad
Stage 5, page 146

Creamy Tomato Soup
Stage 1, page 96

DINNER

Scallops Piccata
Stage 6, page 160

SNACKS

Seasonal Mixed-Berry Crostata
Stage 6, page 166

Chicken Muffins
Stage 4, page 131

ONE-WEEK SAMPLE MEAL PLAN

MONDAY	TUESDAY	WEDNESDAY	THURSDAY	FRIDAY	SATURDAY
Liver-Loving Juice Stage 4, page 133 **Roasted Butternut Squash Pancakes** Stage 3, page 124	**Green Goddess Juice** Stage 4, page 132 **Sauerkraut Scramble** Stage 3, page 120	**Liver-Loving Juice** Stage 4, page 133 **Asparagus Fried Eggs** Stage 3, page 122	**Green Goddess Juice** Stage 4, page 132 **Easy Avocado Omelette** Stage 3, page 125	**Peppery Pear Juice** Stage 4, page 132 **Sauerkraut Scramble** Stage 3, page 120	**Santa Fe Breakfast Tostadas** Stage 3, page 121
Beetroot and Beef Short Rib Borscht Stage 1, page 98	**Roasted Brussels Sprout Apple Salad** Stage 6, page 159 **Three-Onion Soup** Stage 1, page 93	**Beetroot and Beef Short Rib Borscht** Stage 1, page 98	**Chicken Thigh Puttanesca** Stage 6, page 163	**Braised Beef Burgers** Stage 2, page 108	**Chicken-Stuffed Cabbage Rolls** Stage 2, page 111
Pan Steak with Mushrooms Stage 1, page 102	**Chicken Thigh Puttanesca** Stage 6, page 163	**Braised Beef Burgers** Stage 2, page 108	**Roasted Butternut Squash Pancakes** Stage 3, page 124 **Scrambled eggs** Stage 3	**Chicken-Stuffed Cabbage Rolls** Stage 2, page 111	**Roasted Brussels Sprout Apple Salad** Stage 6, page 159 **Three-Onion Soup** Stage 1, page 93
Dairy-Free Key Lime Mousse Stage 6, page 164 **Peppery Pear Juice** Stage 4, page 132	**Honey Bombs** Stage 6, page 168 **Anytime Smoothie** Stage 6, page 158	**Baked Cinnamon Walnut Apples** Stage 5, page 155 **Green Goddess Juice** Stage 4, page 132	**Olive Raisin Tapenade** Stage 6, page 162 **Guacamole** Stage 5, page 150	**Anytime Smoothie** Stage 6, page 158 **Apple Pie Stewed Apples** Stage 5, page 154	**Gingered Vanilla Honey Drops** Stage 6, page 169 **Crackling Nuts** Stage 4, page 143

The Full Diet

FULL DIET

You've made it through the introduction diet. Not only are you feeling better, but you're also reaping the rewards of a healthy gut, ranging from hormonal balance and reduced inflammation to better emotional and mental wellbeing.

How This Stage Works

- **Expanded menu** On the full diet, your food choices are greater. Visit gapsdiet.com for specifics on what you can eat and what you should continue to avoid.

- **Balance** Take it easy on desserts and starchier carbs. Your microbiome is delicately balanced, and too much of anything can give opportunistic bacteria the upper hand.

- **Symptom control** You can repeat the introduction diet once a year, or whenever you feel symptoms beginning to reoccur.

What You Can Expect

- **New foods** Take care when adding new foods, maintain your food journal, and wait a few days between additions to see how your body responds.

- **Plan ahead** Before going out to eat or to a party, get some idea of what you'll be able to eat. Make sure there will be something acceptable, so you don't jeopardize your healing.

- **Temptation** Wanting to eat foods that aren't GAPS legal is normal. Remember where you came from, and stay strong. If you go back to eating the way you used to eat, you'll eventually find yourself right back where you started.

Salmon Spinach Cobb Salad is a no-cook recipe you can make to add variety to your menu and increase your vegetable intake.

Lemon Almond Flour Biscotti offer great crunch and pair well with a soothing cup of tea.

What You Can Eat

VEGETABLES Cooked and raw vegetables are now a bigger part of your diet. More fibrous vegetables also make a comeback, as your range increases.

- **Versatile veg** Add back swede, rhubarb, aubergine, and peppers, as well as seaweed.

- **Some beans, groundnuts and pulses** Try lentils, haricot beans, split peas, peanuts, and peanut butter.

FRUIT The range of fruit is much greater now, so you can enjoy stronger flavours and textures.

- **Citrus** Add kumquats, grapefruit, limes, oranges, tangerines, and satsumas.

- **Tropical fruits** Liven up your meals with mangoes, pineapple, and papaya.

- **Old favourites** Other fruits also make a return, including melons, grapes, and even olives.

DAIRY If you tolerate it, dairy is another expanded category, allowing more varied cheeses.

- **Family favourites** Now you can enjoy Cheddar, Emmental, Monterey Jack, and similar cheeses.

- **Slicing cheeses** Havarti, Edam, and Gouda melt well and can boost the flavour of your meals.

- **Harder cheeses** Asiago, Pecorino, and Parmesan grate well and can expand your salad horizons.

- **Softer, stronger cheeses** Blue cheeses such as Gorgonzola, Stilton, and Roquefort, as well as Brie, Camembert, and Port du Salut, now join the menu.

> **SUPPLEMENTS**
> Continue with probiotics, cod liver oil, HCl, and ox bile (if you need it), adjusting as necessary. You can opt to work with a certified GAPS practitioner if you think you need help fine-tuning your supplements.

ALCOHOL On occasion, small amounts of alcohol are allowable. One drink at a celebratory occasion is one thing; a cocktail every night can cause a relapse. Explore naturally fermented beverages such as kombucha, which help maintain gut health instead of disturbing it.

- **Spirits** You can enjoy an occasional cocktail with gin or a dram of whisky.

- **Wine** A glass of dry red or white wine with a meal now and then is allowed.

Parmesan Rosemary Tuiles are easy-to-make, low-lactose crisps you can pair with your favourite dip.

Meal Plan

You're now full GAPS legal, but it's no time to get complacent. To maintain your gut health progress, it's important to keep moving forward. Focus on increasing variety as you plan your meals, continue to challenge your kitchen skills, and maximize your nutrient intake potential to nourish your gut and body.

NEW STAGE-SPECIFIC CHOICES and recommendations include the following:

- **Probiotic vegetables** Kimchi and Kowabunga Kimchi are new recipes in your fermenting arsenal.

- **Dairy** Continue as tolerated.

- **Mains** Don't be overwhelmed by the number of new choices. Remember what you've learned about planning and preparing, and incorporate a few at a time into your menu.

- **Desserts** In moderation, semi-sweet options like Spiced Carrot Cake, Very Berry "Ice Cream", and Lemon Almond Flour Biscotti go a long way towards satisfying a sweet tooth.

- **Snacks** Pick a few each week to focus on. Spreads and dips can double as sauces and condiments. New choices include Hunger Buster Bars, Nut Butter, Nut Cheese, Parmesan Rosemary Tuiles, Three-Seed Crackers, Cauliflower Hummus, Roasted Aubergine Spread, Garden Fresh Salsa, and Tzatziki Sauce.

Three-Seed Crackers are a crunchy snack you can enjoy with chicken salad or your favourite nut or dairy cheese.

SUNDAY

BREAKFAST

Grilled Vegetable Frittata
Full diet, page 177

LUNCH

Calming Kale Salad
Full diet, page 180

Creamy Tomato Soup
Stage 1, page 96

DINNER

Tiger Prawn and Cauliflower Grits
Full diet, page 199

SNACKS

Tea or stock
Stage 1

Very Berry "Ice Cream"
Full diet, page 212

Lemon Almond Flour Biscotti
Full diet, page 214

ONE-WEEK SAMPLE MEAL PLAN

MONDAY	TUESDAY	WEDNESDAY	THURSDAY	FRIDAY	SATURDAY
Grainless Granola Full diet, page 176 **Nut Milk** Stage 4, page 71	**Grilled Vegetable Frittata** Full diet, page 177	**Grainless Granola** Full diet, page 176 **Nut Milk** Stage 4, page 71	**Sausage, Egg, and Cheese Sandwich** Full diet, page 173	**Grainless Granola** Full diet, page 176 **Nut Milk** Stage 4, page 71	**Cheddar Chive Biscuits with Sausage Gravy** Full diet, page 174
Grilled Vegetable Frittata Full diet, page 177	**Chopped Cobb Salad** Full diet, page 178 **Creamy Tomato Soup** Stage 1, page 96	**Oven-Roasted Moroccan Chicken with Morrocan Cauliflower "Couscous"** Full diet, page 196	**Tuna Cakes with Rémoulade** Full diet, page 195 **Slammin' Hot Slaw** Full diet, page 198	**Vegetable Beef Stewp** Stage 2, page 107	**Margherita Pizza** Full diet, page 194
Lamb Burger Sliders Full diet, page 192 **Kimchi** Full diet, page 200	**Oven-Roasted Moroccan Chicken with Morrocan Cauliflower "Couscous"** Full diet, page 196	**Tuna Cakes with Rémoulade** Full diet, page 195 **Slammin' Hot Slaw** Full diet, page 198	**Vegetable Beef Stewp** Stage 2, page 107	**Margherita Pizza** Full diet, page 194	**Asparagus Fried Eggs** Stage 3, page 122
Tea or stock Stage 1 **Nut Butter, Nut Cheese, or dairy cheese with Three-Seed Crackers** Full diet, pages 208, 209, 206 **Green Goddess Juice** Stage 4, page 132	**Tea or stock** Stage 1 **Hunger Buster Bars** Full diet, page 211 **Anytime Smoothie** Stage 6, page 158	**Tea or stock** Stage 1 **Roasted Aubergine Spread with Parmesan Rosemary Tuiles** Full diet, pages 202, 204 **Baked Cinnamon Walnut Apples** Stage 5, page 155	**Tea or stock** Stage 1 **Liver-Loving Juice** Stage 4, page 133 **Seasonal Mixed-Berry Crostada** Stage 6, page 166	**Tea or stock** Stage 1 **Hunger Buster Bars** Full diet, page 211 **Olive Raisin Tapenade** Stage 6, page 162 **Parmesan Rosemary Tuiles** Full diet, page 204	**Tea or stock** Stage 1 **Peppery Pear Juice** Stage 4, page 132 **Cauliflower Hummus** Full diet, page 202 **Three-Seed Crackers** Full diet, page 206

Going Forward

After transitioning into the full GAPS diet, many people wonder when they can go back to their old way of eating. The short answer is never. The full GAPS diet is intended to become your everyday way of eating. Once dysbiosis has been established in your gut, you'll generally always need to avoid certain foods, such as refined sugars and grains, especially if you had a severe condition. The good news is that there are many more foods you can eat compared to those you can't. Here are a few things to keep in mind as you move forward.

Milestone 1 The 80/20 Rule

3–6 MONTHS INTO THE DIET Most people try to shoot for 80 per cent GAPS, 20 per cent "cheating" in their menu. Bear in mind, if you're cheating with high-trigger foods like sugar and grains, you definitely run the risk of a full relapse. You'll probably find that the risk isn't worth it. Stay alert to digestive changes, and if a digestive flare-up is severe, you might want to go back to Stage 1 or 2 for a few days to let things settle down again. Most people find that with the wide variety of delicious foods available, it's better to stick with full GAPS and enjoy a symptom-free life.

Milestone 2 Testing Food Intolerances

6 MONTHS INTO THE DIET By now you've determined your food allergies, sensitivities, and intolerances. After about 6 months of symptom-free eating, you might want to try reintroducing foods you were sensitive to. Begin by trying the Food Sensitivity Test (see right). If there is no irritation, try a small amount of the food and wait to see if any of your symptoms return. If you're still sensitive, continue to avoid the food.

Braised Beef Burgers are a tasty, juicy, and healing burger option.

Milestone 3 Reintroducing Dairy

6 MONTHS INTO THE DIET If you previously had a dairy intolerance, you might want to try reintroducing dairy after 6 months on the full GAPS diet with no digestive symptoms. Here's how:

1 Start by using ghee.

2 If you have no digestive flare-ups for 6 weeks, move on to butter.

3 If butter is tolerated, try home-made cultured cream. Start slowly, with 1 or 2 tablespoons, and build up to 240–475ml (8–16fl oz) per day, again waiting 6 weeks and looking for any signs of digestive distress.

4 The next step is kefir, using the same method of starting with 1 or 2 tablespoons and increasing to 240–475ml (8–16fl oz) per day.

5 If you tolerate kefir, you can try Cheddar or Parmesan cheese, adding a small amount to a meal and seeing how you react over the next 3–5 days.

6 If all goes well, you can begin to add other GAPS-legal cheeses, always using your food journal to record what effect the new foods may have on your body.

If, along this path, you react to any food, eliminate it and do not progress any further. You can always try again in another 6 months. Your gut might need more healing time, or it could be that you have a true allergy to dairy rather than an intolerance. Consult a medical professional if you suspect this is the case.

Milestone 4 Doing Another Intro

1 YEAR INTO THE DIET Many people choose to do a round of the introduction diet once or twice a year to shore up their gut lining, which can be compromised by abuse of the 80/20 rule or by other stressors. You can repeat the intro diet as often as needed, taking time off between to enjoy the full GAPS diet. Keep in mind that prolonged restricted diets can put you in danger of getting bored and frustrated and falling into binge behaviour, which will make things worse rather than better.

Food Sensitivity Test

SKIN TEST

To test for a food sensitivity, follow these steps. (This works best with liquid foods.)

1 Put a drop of the test food on the inside of your forearm before going to bed. If it's a solid food, mix it with a bit of water.

2 Leave the food overnight, and check the spot the next morning. If it's red and irritated, it's most likely not tolerated.

PULSE TEST

Alternatively, you can do a pulse test. (This is handy for foods that aren't easy to skin test.)

1 Sit down, take a deep breath, and record your pulse rate for 1 full minute.

2 Take a bite of the food in question and chew it (but do not swallow it) for 30 seconds.

3 Take your pulse again for another full minute.

4 If your pulse rate has increased by 6 beats or more, the food is likely not tolerated. Spit out the food, rinse your mouth, and wait for your 1-minute pulse reading to return to normal before testing other foods.

Foundation Recipes and Basics

The recipes and techniques in this part are the building blocks for the diet and its stages. Master these ferments, cultures, stocks, broths, and more, and you'll be prepared to tackle the diet with minimal stress.

DAIRY FREE **NUT FREE** **PALEO DIET**

Meat Stock

There's no contest between highly processed, commercially available stocks and bouillons and the home-made version. Warm and mildly meaty, home-made stock is natural and contains the minerals, vitamins, and amino acids needed to support gut health and digestion in an easy-to-process form.

Prep Time
15 minutes

Cook Time
3–5 hours

Makes
8 servings

INGREDIENTS

2.25kg (5lb) beef or lamb shanks

6 carrots, roughly chopped

6 celery sticks, roughly chopped

2 onions, roughly chopped

6 garlic cloves

5 sprigs of rosemary

5 sprigs of thyme

3 tsp sea salt

8 whole black peppercorns

2 litres (3½ pints) water

METHOD

1 In a large stockpot, combine the beef shanks, carrots, celery, onions, garlic, rosemary, thyme, sea salt, black peppercorns, and water. Place over a medium-high heat and bring to the boil.

2 Cover, reduce the heat to medium-low, and simmer for 3–5 hours. Remove the bones and meat, and set aside.

3 Strain the stock through a fine sieve into a large pan and cool the stock.

4 Separate the meat from the bones, and store the cooled meat and bones in the fridge, tightly covered, to use in broths and meals.

5 Pour the broth into jars with tight-sealing lids and keep in the fridge for up to 7 days, or freeze for up to 6 months.

STAGE 1

 DAIRY FREE

 NUT FREE

 PALEO DIET

Chicken Stock

Chicken stock makes a great base and an easy flavour-enhancer for many dishes, including soups, stews, and casseroles. It's also warm, filling, and nourishing all on its own.

Prep Time
10 minutes

Cook Time
2 hours

Makes
16 servings

INGREDIENTS

1 roasting chicken, about 2.25kg (5lb)

1 large carrot, unpeeled, chopped

1 large celery stick, chopped

1 large onion, skin on, chopped

1 bay leaf

10 sprigs of thyme

1 tbsp black peppercorns

1 tsp sea salt

5.5 litres (9½ pints) water

METHOD

1 In a large stockpot, combine the chicken, carrot, celery, onion, bay leaf, thyme, black peppercorns, sea salt, and water. Place over a high heat and bring to the boil.

2 Reduce the heat to low, and simmer uncovered for 2 hours.

3 Remove the chicken from the pot, and strain the stock through a fine sieve into a large pan.

4 Pull the cooked chicken from the bones, cool, and store in the fridge, tightly covered, for future use.

5 If not using immediately, place the stock pan in the sink and surround it with cold water and ice cubes to cool.

6 Store in a container with a tight-sealing lid for up to 7 days in the fridge, or freeze for up to 6 months.

Variations

Roasted Chicken Stock

STAGE 4

Roast the chicken first to yield a richer, deeper-flavoured stock. Preheat the oven to 190°C (375°F/Gas 5), place the chicken on a baking tray or in a roasting dish, and roast for 30 minutes, or until the skin is browned. The chicken won't be fully cooked at this point. Transfer it, along with any browned bits and juices from the roasting pan, to a large stockpot. Add the remaining ingredients and follow the rest of the recipe.

Roast chicken is a good place to start your stock in the later stages, resulting in a more flavourful dish.

Fish Stock

Substitute 2kg (4lb) fish for the chicken, and simmer for no more than 45 minutes. Use the bones, skins, and heads, in place of the meat. For a lighter-flavoured stock, choose a mild white fish, such as halibut, sole, flounder, or turbot. For a stronger-tasting stock, use salmon.

STAGE 1

FULL DIET

DAIRY FREE **NUT FREE** **PALEO DIET**

Beef Bone Broth

Once you've transitioned to the full diet, you can replace stock with bone broth in your soups and for sipping between meals. Cooked over a longer time, bone broth is full of minerals and stomach-healing gelatine.

Prep Time
1¼ hours

Cook Time
24–72 hours

Makes
16 servings

INGREDIENTS

- 4 litres (6½ pints) spring or filtered water
- 120ml (4fl oz) cider vinegar
- 1 beef knuckle and marrow bones, about 1.5–2kg (3–4lb)
- 1kg (2lb) meaty bones, such as oxtail or short ribs
- 2 celery sticks, chopped into thirds
- 2 large carrots, coarsely chopped
- 2 onions, cut into quarters
- Unrefined sea salt (no additives)

METHOD

1 In a large stockpot, combine the spring water, cider vinegar, beef knuckle and marrow bones, and meaty bones, adding more water if needed to completely cover the bones.

2 Add the celery, carrots, and onions. Place over a high heat and bring to the boil, skimming any scum off the top as needed.

3 Reduce the heat to medium-low, cover, and simmer for 24–72 hours. (You can use a slow cooker for this if you like.) The longer the broth simmers, the more gelatine is released.

4 Strain the broth through a fine sieve. Return any bone marrow to the broth, season with salt, then cool.

5 Pour the broth into heatproof jars with tight-sealing lids, and keep in the fridge for up to 7 days, or freeze for up to 6 months.

Variation

Chicken Bone Broth

Replace the beef bones with 1 chicken, about 1.5–2kg (3–4lb), free-range and organic if possible; 2–4 chicken feet; and 1 chicken neck (optional). Then proceed with the recipe as directed.

Fermenting Basics

Fermented or cultured vegetables are an integral part of the gut-healing process because they repopulate the gut with beneficial bacteria, which help restore balance to your microbiome. Any vegetable can be fermented.

Choose Organic

Choose organic vegetables if possible. Fermenting increases the vitamin and mineral content of the vegetables, so it's good to start with vegetables at the peak of freshness.

- Cabbage is the most popular vegetable used for fermentation.

- Turnips and other root vegetables ferment well.

- Vegetables such as peppers or carrots can be added for colour and flavour. Experiment to find out what you like.

Sterilize Your Equipment

It's essential all your jars and utensils are clean before fermenting. You're creating a bacteria-friendly environment, so it's important no undesirable bacteria remain that could multiply.

- Pulling jars directly out of the dishwasher after the drying cycle ensures sterility.

- To be completely confident, you can submerge your jars and utensils in boiling water to sterilize them.

- It's more likely that the good bacteria will crowd out any bad bacteria, but it's better to be safe than sorry.

Simple Sauerkraut

You can use these steps to ferment other vegetables as well.

INGREDIENTS

1 head of cabbage
1 tbsp sea salt
spring or filtered
   water

1 Remove the outer 2 or 3 leaves from the cabbage, and slice the cabbage thinly using a chef's knife.

2 Place the sliced cabbage in a large bowl. With clean hands, begin to work the cabbage, squeezing and massaging it until it starts to release liquid. (This is called the brine.)

Culturing Tips

Keep these tips in mind when you're culturing vegetables.

- Vegetables culture at room temperature, so find a place where they can sit out of direct sunlight for at least 7 days.

- For a more sour taste, continue fermenting, testing each week. When your desired flavour is reached, move the jar to the fridge to slow the fermentation.

- The more sour the taste, the more beneficial bacteria are present. You might find that your taste buds change and your body begins to crave these friendly microbes.

- Glass jars and plastic lids are easy to find online or at your local supermarket or hardware shop.

- Make sure you have large bowls to accommodate the vegetables as you shred and mix them.

- You can use a spatula or spoon to pack the vegetables into the jars. No fancy equipment is needed.

NO FERMENTED FRUIT

You can ferment fruits as well as vegetables, although more care must be taken when working with fruits, because the sugar in them produces small amounts of alcohol when fermented. Fermented fruit is not appropriate for a gut-healing diet.

3 Tightly pack the shredded cabbage into 1-litre (1³/₄ pint) glass jars. Use your hands, a spatula, or any sturdy kitchen tool to press down firmly. Add sea salt.

4 Use a small glass to pack down the cabbage one last time, leaving 5cm (2in) breathing space at the top of the jar. Add the lid, close firmly, and then loosen a quarter-turn.

5 If the cabbage has not produced enough brine on its own, fill the jar with water until the cabbage is completely submerged. Let the jars sit at room temperature out of direct sunlight for 7 days. "Burp" the jars each day by opening the lids, closing firmly, then loosening a quarter-turn. Taste the sauerkraut after 7 days. For more of a sour flavour, ferment for up to 2 weeks. Store in the fridge for up to 6 months.

STAGE 3

DAIRY FREE

LOW FODMAP

Red Cabbage Kraut

Crisp and tangy, this colourful 7-day ferment recipe is rich in probiotics, vitamins, and minerals that support gut health. Use the juice in Stages 1 and 2 and the cabbage itself in Stage 3.

Prep Time
20 minutes

Cook Time
7 days

Makes
2 1-litre (1³/₄-pint) jars

INGREDIENTS

60g (2oz) unrefined sea salt (no additives)

1.8 litres (3¹/₄ pints) filtered mineral water

1 head of red cabbage, stemmed, cored, and finely shredded

METHOD

1 In a medium bowl, dissolve the sea salt in the water.

2 Pack the red cabbage tightly into 2 glass jars. Pour the brine into the jars over the cabbage, packing down the cabbage so it's completely submerged, and leaving 2.5–5cm (1–2in) space at the top.

3 Cover the jars with the lids, and set aside at room temperature out of direct sunlight for 7 days.

4 Once daily, loosen the lids to allow the gases to escape. Press down on the cabbage as needed to ensure it remains submerged in brine. Retighten the lids.

5 Keep in the fridge for up to 6 months.

Variation

Sweet-and-Sour Red Slaw

STAGE 6

Combine around 75g (2½oz) Red Cabbage Kraut with ½ red apple, sliced; ½ carrot, grated; 1 tablespoon of raisins; 1 tablespoon of walnuts; and 1 tablespoon of extra virgin olive oil.

Sweet-and-Sour Red Slaw

DAIRY FREE

NUT FREE

PALEO DIET

Fermented Mixed Vegetables

In this gut-healing giardiniera, brightly coloured, mild-flavoured vegetables make a great standalone snack or a perfect condiment for meat, fish, or eggs. Incorporate the juice starting in Stage 1, and add the vegetables when you get to Stage 3.

Prep Time
15 minutes

Cook Time
6 days

Makes
8 servings

INGREDIENTS

- 2 tbsp unrefined sea salt (no additives)
- 1 litre (1¾ pints) filtered mineral water
- 2 carrots, about 150g (5½oz) in total, cut into 1cm (½in) rounds
- 1 large yellow pepper, ribs and seeds removed, and cut into 2.5cm (1in) squares
- 1 large red pepper, ribs and seeds removed, and cut into 2.5cm (1in) squares
- 140g (5oz) cauliflower florets, cut into 2.5cm (1in) pieces
- 4 garlic cloves, halved

METHOD

1 In a small bowl, dissolve the sea salt in the water.

2 Using a wooden spoon, tightly pack the carrot, yellow and red pepper, cauliflower, and garlic into a 1-litre glass jar. Add the water, leaving 2.5–5cm (1–2in) space at the top of the jar. Press down on the vegetables, if necessary, to completely submerge them.

3 Place the lid on the jar, and set aside at room temperature out of direct sunlight for 6 days.

4 Once daily, loosen the lid to allow gases to escape. Press down on the vegetables as needed to ensure they remain submerged. Retighten the lid.

5 Keep in the fridge for up to 6 months.

Yellow peppers

STAGE 4

 DAIRY FREE

 NUT FREE

 PALEO DIET

Cultured Spring Vegetables

Probiotic-rich cultured vegetables help rebalance gut flora. Start with small amounts of juice in Stages 1 and 2, and slowly build up to 2–4 tablespoons of vegetables with each meal in Stage 3.

Prep Time
20 minutes

Cook Time
6 days

Makes
4 1-litre jars

INGREDIENTS

1 green cabbage
1 yellow squash, such as yellow courgette or patty pan
1 courgette
2 large carrots
300g (10oz) kale, thinly sliced
4 tsp sea salt
Spring or filtered water

METHOD

1 In a food processor fitted with a chopping blade, shred the green cabbage, yellow squash, courgette, and carrots.

2 Transfer the shredded vegetables to a large bowl, add the kale, and stir to combine.

3 Pack the vegetables into four 1-litre glass jars, pressing down firmly with a spatula. Leave 5–7.5cm (2–3in) at the top of each jar.

4 Add 1 teaspoon of sea salt to each jar, and fill with water to completely submerge. Seal tightly.

5 Let the jars sit at room temperature, out of direct sunlight, for 6 days.

6 Store in the fridge for up to 6 months.

Variations

Cultured Root Vegetables

 STAGE 4

Replace the yellow squash with 1 beetroot, and instead of the courgette, use 1 turnip. Decrease the kale to 150g (5oz), and add 150g (5oz) radishes. Shred the beetroot, turnip, and radishes, and combine with the other vegetables.

Cultured Rainbow Vegetables

STAGE 4

Use red cabbage. Replace the yellow squash with 2 yellow peppers, ribs and seeds removed, and instead of the courgette, use 2 orange peppers, ribs and seeds removed. Decrease the kale to 150g (5oz), and add 2 red peppers, ribs and seeds removed. Shred the peppers, and combine with the other vegetables as directed.

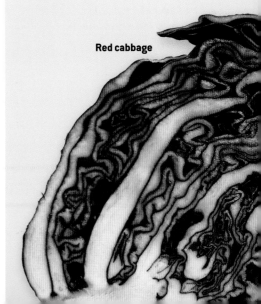

Red cabbage

LOW FODMAP

NUT FREE

Home-Churned Butter

It's hard to beat the silky texture and rich flavour of fresh, home-made butter – you'll never choose shop-bought butter again. This easy recipe provides the foundation for home-made ghee as well.

Prep Time
15 minutes

Makes
about 450g (1lb)

INGREDIENTS

1 litre (1 ³/₄ pints) organic, unpasteurized double cream, or organic, lightly pasteurized, unhomogenized double cream

METHOD

1 Using a food processor fitted with a metal blade, a blender, or a mixer fitted with a metal whisk attachment, whip the cream at a low speed. Increase the speed to medium as the cream starts to thicken.

2 When the cream has solidified into butter and liquid forms in the bowl, stop whipping. Discard the liquid.

3 Transfer the butter to the middle of a piece of cheesecloth large enough to wrap it completely. Wash the wrapped butter in cold water, squeezing the butter as you rinse, until the water runs clear.

4 Pack the butter in an airtight container, or wrap in cling film or a plastic bag, and keep in the fridge for several weeks or freeze for up to 9 months.

NUT FREE   **LOW FODMAP**

Ghee

With a rich, nutty taste, and no milk solids or lactose to cause intolerances, ghee is ideal for those with sensitivity to dairy products. Use it as you would butter. It's also a good addition to soups and broths for some extra gut-healing fat.

Prep Time
2 minutes

Cook Time
20–30 minutes

Makes
scant 450g (1lb)

INGREDIENTS

450g (1lb) unsalted butter

METHOD

1 In a medium saucepan over a medium heat, melt the butter for 10–15 minutes.

2 As the butter begins to bubble, reduce the heat to medium-low. Skim off foam as it develops, and cook for another 10–15 minutes, allowing browned milk solids to form and drop to the bottom of the pan.

3 Strain the ghee through a fine sieve lined with cheesecloth into an airtight, heatproof container.

4 Store at room temperature for up to 6 months.

Ghee

❝ You can also cook the butter in a slow cooker on low for 6–8 hours. Skim off the foam if desired, or allow it to sink to the bottom. Strain as directed. ❞

STAGE 4

DAIRY FREE   PALEO DIET

Nut Milk

If you can't tolerate dairy, nut milk is an excellent alternative. And by making it yourself, you can avoid unwanted sugars and chemicals, and maximize your nutrient absorption.

Prep Time
15 minutes

Makes
750ml–1 litre
(1¼–1¾ pints)

INGREDIENTS

- 140g (5oz) nuts, soaked overnight
- 1 litre (1¾ pints) very hot spring or filtered water

METHOD

1 In a high-speed blender, blend the nuts and hot water for 2 minutes.

2 Transfer the mixture to a nut milk bag or a fine sieve lined with cheesecloth, and gently squeeze the bag or press down on the solids to strain the milk into a bowl. Thin the milk with more spring water if needed to achieve the desired consistency.

3 Keep in a glass jar in the fridge for up to 3 days.

Variations

Coconut Milk

STAGE 6

Use 1.2 litres (2 pints) very hot water, and replace the nuts with 225g (8oz) unsweetened coconut flakes. Blend for 3 minutes, and then proceed as directed.

Flavoured Nut Milk

FULL DIET

When you reach the full diet stage, you can make your nut milk a little more interesting by adding spices or sweeteners. Try adding cinnamon, nutmeg, or honey after step 2.

Coconut

Cultured Dairy Basics

Cultured dairy helps repopulate your gut with beneficial bacteria that restore balance to your microbiome. Milk and cream can be cultured in a variety of ways for a different tastes and results.

THE IMPORTANCE OF STERILIZATION

Dairy should be cultured in clean, dry glass jars so that no opportunistic bacteria can spoil the culture. Using jars straight out of the dishwasher is ideal. You can sterilize jars in boiling water for 30–60 seconds if you suspect they might be contaminated. Make sure your utensils are also clean and dry.

Kefir

Kefir is a sour-tasting drink made of cow's or goat's milk.

- Kefir has the highest quantity of beneficial bacteria and yeast among cultured dairy products.

- It contains kefirans, which have shown potential as anticancer agents in scientific research.

- Home-made kefir includes the full complement of bacteria and yeast that commercial versions lack.

Cultured Dairy

Cultured dairy is simple to make, although you might need to make adjustments based on the temperature in your kitchen. It'll be worth it, however.

INGREDIENTS

950ml (1³/₄ pints) organic, grass-fed raw or lightly pasteurized/ unhomogenized whole milk

2 tbsp organic commercial yogurt, or powdered starter

1 Heat the milk to about 32°C (90°F) to activate the cultures. If you're using raw milk, you can scald it by heating it to 82°C (180°F) to kill any native beneficial bacteria that can change the flavour. If you do this, don't add the starter until the temperature drops to 32°C (90°F).

2 Add 1–2 tablespoons of finished yogurt to the heated milk, or use a dried starter culture. (The first time you use a dried starter, you might need additional time for culturing because the culture is waking up after having been dried. Jars should be clean and dry.)

Yogurt

Yogurt, the most familiar cultured dairy product, is slightly thicker than kefir.

- By law, yogurt should contain *Lactobacillus bulgaricus* and/or *Streptococcus thermophilus*.

- There are two types of yogurt starter: thermophilic (heat-loving) starter and mesophilic starter, which does not need to be heated.

- Home-made yogurt won't be as thick as commercially made yogurt. To thicken it, you can strain it through layers of cheesecloth in a sieve over a bowl. Pour in the yogurt, and allow it to sit for several hours or until it reaches the desired consistency.

Cultured Cream and Butter

Cultured cream and butter are healthy products that provide both flavour and nutrients.

- The higher the fat content of the cream, the thicker your cultured cream will be. If you want thicker cultured cream, scald the cream and let it cool for 30 minutes before culturing.

- Butter made with milk from cows who have grazed on grass has a rich, golden colour that indicates its high nutrient content.

- Both cream and butter are excellent sources of vitamins A, D, E, and K, as well as cholesterol, which is the building block of every cell in your body.

BUYING DAIRY FOR CULTURING

You can make cultured dairy products with raw or pasteurized milk. Raw milk has many health benefits. The natural bacteria in milk may slightly alter the taste of the finished product as they interact with the culture that's been added. If you're buying pasteurized milk, try to get milk that's been lightly pasteurized, and avoid ultra-pasteurized (UHT) milk. The proteins in this type of milk have been denatured and have lost much of their vitality. Avoid homogenized milk, too; its fats are difficult to assimilate.

3 Allow the dairy product to cool to room temperature. Then, let the cultures sit at room temperature, out of direct sunlight, for 24 hours. The temperature of your kitchen has a big impact on the culturing time. If your kitchen is cool, you can culture your jars in a cooler, as above.

4 Cover the jars in the cooler with a blanket or towel to maintain the right temperature. If your dairy product separates before 24 hours, you might need less time due to a warmer kitchen, or you might have used too much starter.

STAGE 1

NUT FREE

Yogurt

Tangy, silky yogurt is easy to make and much healthier than shop-bought versions. In later stages of the diet, you can add soaked and dried nuts or unsweetened, flaked coconut, and season with cinnamon, nutmeg, and pure vanilla extract.

Prep Time
2 minutes

Cook Time
24 hours

Makes
8 servings

INGREDIENTS

950ml (1³/₄ pints) organic, raw or lightly pasteurized unhomogenized whole milk

60ml (2fl oz) organic commercial yogurt

METHOD

1 In a medium saucepan over a low heat, heat the milk for about 10 minutes, or until it reaches 80°C (180°F). (Use a thermometer.) If you're using raw milk, heat it to 40°C (110°F).

2 Remove from the heat, and allow the milk to cool for about 10 minutes, or until it reaches 40°C (110°F).

3 Place the yogurt in a 1-litre glass jar with a tight-fitting lid, and fill the jar with warm milk, leaving 2.5cm (1in) space at the top.

4 Place the jar in a yogurt maker or a dehydrator set to 40°C (110°F), or in the oven with the light on for 24 hours.

5 Allow the yogurt to cool in the fridge.

Variations

Coconut Milk Yogurt

STAGE 3

Substitute one 400ml can of coconut milk for the organic whole milk. Shake the can vigorously before opening. Add 1 probiotic capsule to the coconut milk, and culture as directed.

Almond Milk Yogurt

STAGE 3

Substitute 950ml (1³/₄ pints) almond milk for the organic whole milk. After heating the milk, add 1 tablespoon of raw honey and 1 or 2 probiotic capsules. Culture milk as directed.

Almond milk

Cultured Cream

Cultured cream, or what many people think of as soured cream, is an excellent addition to soups if you can tolerate dairy. If you've been using low-fat soured cream, this will be all the tastier.

Prep Time	Cook Time	Makes
5 minutes	24–48 hours	950ml (1¾ pints)

INGREDIENTS

950ml (1¾ pints) organic raw, or lightly pasteurized, unhomogenized cream

60ml (2fl oz) yogurt, previously made cultured cream, or yogurt starter

METHOD

1 In a large saucepan over a medium heat, heat the cream to 85°C (185°F), and maintain this temperature for 45 minutes, watching the thermometer carefully.

2 Remove from the heat, and let the cream cool to 25°C (77°F).

3 Pour the cooled cream into a glass jar with a tight-fitting lid. Add the yogurt.

4 Seal the jar, and set aside out of direct sunlight for 24 hours. If your kitchen is cooler than 23°C (74°F), place the jars in a cooler with the lid closed while culturing.

5 Check the cream for consistency. If it's not thick enough, set aside for up to 48 hours.

Variations

Cultured Butter

Follow the Cultured Cream instructions. After the cream has cultured, chill it in the fridge until it has cooled to 15°C (60°F). Proceed as directed in the Home-Churned Butter recipe.

Crème Fraîche

Use 60ml (2fl oz) shop-bought cultured buttermilk instead of yogurt, previously made cultured cream, or a yogurt starter.

NUT FREE

Kefir

Kefir is a powerhouse of probiotics. Given its tart taste, you might want to sweeten it with honey. Whatever your preference, your gut will thank you for making it a regular part of your diet.

Prep Time
5 minutes

Cook Time
24 hours

Makes
8 servings

INGREDIENTS

- 950ml (1¾ pints) organic raw or lightly pasteurized, unhomogenized whole milk
- 1 packet kefir starter or 2 tbsp kefir grains

METHOD

1. In a medium saucepan over a medium heat, heat the milk to 82°C (180°F), using a thermometer. If you're using raw milk, heat to 40°C (110°F).

2. Cool the milk to 40°C (110°F). If necessary, place the pan in the sink and surround with cold water and ice cubes to cool it quickly. Pour into a 1-litre glass jar, along with the kefir starter.

3. Seal the jar and set aside at room temperature, out of direct sunlight, for 24 hours. Occasionally shake the jar to ensure all the milk is fermenting.

4. Strain the kefir into a fresh jar, and use the grains to start another batch. If using a starter, reserve 120ml (4fl oz) kefir to start the next batch.

Variations

Coconut Milk Kefir

STAGE 6

Substitute 950ml (1¾ pints) coconut milk for the whole milk if you can't tolerate dairy. Do not heat the coconut milk. Proceed as described.

Flavoured Kefir

STAGE 6

Use a second fermentation. Add about 30g (1oz) of your favourite fruit to the jar, cap tightly, and let ferment at room temperature for another 24 hours.

Fresh berries

DAIRY FREE   PALEO DIET

Everyday Grain-Free Bread

You'll be glad zero grain doesn't mean zero bread after tasting a slice of this loaf. Because this nutty bread is so nourishing, it's no problem reaching for a second slice, especially with a spread of home-made butter.

Prep Time
15 minutes

Cook Time
40 minutes

Makes
14 servings

INGREDIENTS

6 large eggs

55g (2oz) coconut oil

$\frac{1}{2}$ tsp cider vinegar

190g (6$\frac{1}{2}$oz) smooth almond butter

2 tbsp raw honey

28g (1oz) hazelnut flour/ meal

30g (1oz) home-made coconut flour

1 tsp baking soda

$\frac{3}{4}$ tsp sea salt

METHOD

1 Preheat the oven to 180°C (350°F/Gas 4). Line a 21 ×13cm (8$\frac{1}{2}$ x 4$\frac{1}{2}$in) loaf tin with baking parchment, so the paper extends above the sides by 5cm (2in).

2 In a medium bowl, whisk together the eggs, coconut oil, cider vinegar, almond butter, and honey.

3 In a separate medium bowl, combine the hazelnut flour, coconut flour, baking soda, and sea salt.

4 Gradually add the dry ingredients into the wet ingredients, mixing until well combined, and transfer to the prepared loaf tin.

5 Bake on the middle oven shelf for 45 minutes.

6 Remove the tin from the oven, and allow to cool completely. To remove the bread from the tin, lift the edges of the baking parchment.

Component

Home-made Coconut Flour

Home-made coconut flour is lighter, fluffier, and much lower in fibre than commercial versions. Here's how to make your own.

INGREDIENTS
1 coconut
filtered water

METHOD
1 Remove the thick husk from the coconut until the rounded top is visible. Using a heavy knife, make 4 marks against the top, creating a 5cm (2in) square. Continue to hit against these marks until the coconut opens. Drain out the coconut water.

2 Using a spoon, scrape the coconut meat from the shell, and place in a small bowl. Using a ratio of about 80g (3oz) of meat to 600ml (1 pint) of water, place the coconut and water in a blender, and blend for 1 minute, or until smooth. Strain the blended coconut through a cheesecloth or fine sieve, reserving the coconut milk for another use.

3 Preheat the oven to about 40°C (100°F) – or preheat it to a higher temperature briefly, then turn off. Spread the strained coconut pulp on a baking sheet lined with baking parchment, and bake for 1 hour, or until the moisture has evaporated and the pulp has dried. Allow to cool.

4 Process the cooled, dried coconut pulp in a blender for 30 seconds, or until it's a fine powder. Keep tightly covered in the fridge until needed.

Recipes by Stage

In this part you'll find more than 150 recipes that progress through the diet. From soups to main courses, sides, salads, breakfasts, snacks, desserts, and more, these delicious recipes soothe your gut and provide a satsifying variety of flavours and textures.

STAGE 1

STAGE 5

STAGE 6

FULL
DIET

DAIRY FREE **NUT FREE** **PALEO DIET**

Classic Chicken Soup

This soup is likely to become a go-to meal in Stages 1 and 2. It's quick, easy, tasty, and very good for your gut. Don't forget to add the fat for an extra healing boost.

Prep Time
20 minutes

Cook Time
20 minutes

Makes
8–10 servings

INGREDIENTS

- 2 litres (3½ pints) home-made chicken stock
- 2 carrots, cut into 5mm (¼in) slices
- 2 large celery sticks, cut into 5mm (¼in) slices
- 1 onion, sliced
- 2 tsp sea salt
- 3 or 4 black peppercorns
- 125–250g (4–8oz) cooked, shredded chicken from making stock (optional)
- 2 tbsp animal fat or coconut oil

METHOD

1. In a large stockpot, bring the chicken stock to the boil over a high heat.

2. Reduce the heat to medium-low, and add the carrots, celery, onion, salt, black peppercorns, and chicken (if using). Simmer for 20 minutes. (For earlier stages, you might want to put the peppercorns in a bouquet garni bag or tie them in cheesecloth for easier removal. In Stage 3, you can add 1 tablespoon of finely chopped parsley in the last 5 minutes of cooking. After Stage 4, you can add ½ teaspoon of dried basil.)

3. Serve immediately with 1 or 2 teaspoons of animal fat in each bowl.

Variation

Lemon Chicken "Rice" Soup

STAGE 1

METHOD

1 Replace all the vegetables with ½ head of cauliflower florets, very finely diced (to rice-sized pieces) with a knife or a food processor fitted with a metal chopping blade.

2 After bringing the stock to the boil, reduce the heat to medium-low, add the cauliflower, and cook for 10 minutes. Remove from the heat and add the juice of 2 small lemons.

3 In a medium bowl, whisk 3 egg whites until they form stiff peaks. Fold in 3 beaten egg yolks, and add to the soup a spoonful at a time, mixing well after each spoon. The soup will foam and thicken. Serve immediately.

Cauliflower

DAIRY FREE

NUT FREE

PALEO DIET

Butternut Squash Soup

This warming soup is the perfect comfort food to carry you through the first two stages of the GAPS diet. In later stages, you can add cinnamon, nutmeg, and orange zest.

Variation

Chunky Butternut Kale Soup

STAGE 1

Use 1 peeled, deseeded, and diced butternut squash; 1 large onion, diced; 2 garlic cloves, sliced; 2 carrots, diced; 300g trimmed, chopped kale leaves; 1 tbsp sea salt; and 2 litres (3½ pints) home-made chicken stock. Proceed as directed.

Prep Time
15 minutes

Cook Time
20 minutes

Makes
6–8 servings

INGREDIENTS

- 1 butternut squash, peeled, deseeded, and chopped into 2.5cm (1in) dice
- 1 onion, chopped
- 2 litres (3½ pints) home-made chicken stock
- 1 tbsp sea salt
- 2–3 tbsp coconut oil, lard, butter, or ghee

METHOD

1 In a large stockpot, combine the butternut squash, onion, chicken stock, and sea salt. Place over a high heat and bring to the boil.

2 Reduce the heat to medium-low, and simmer for 20 minutes, or until the squash softens.

3 Working in small batches, blend the soup in a blender until smooth. Return the soup to the pot, and simmer for 5 more minutes, or until the soup has thickened.

4 To serve, add 2–3 teaspoons of coconut oil to each bowl, and ladle the hot soup over to melt.

CHOPPING BUTTERNUT SQUASH

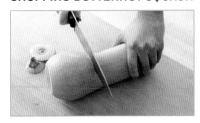

1 Cut off the top and bottom, and slice the squash in half.

2 Remove the skin using a sharp knife or a vegetable peeler.

3 Scoop out the seeds with a spoon and dice the flesh.

DAIRY FREE   NUT FREE   PALEO DIET

Carrot Beetroot Soup

Beetroot aids in the production of bile, which helps you digest all the gut-healing fats you're adding to your diet. This richly coloured soup is also full of antioxidants and phytonutrients – but you won't be thinking about that when you taste its subtle sweetness.

Prep Time
20 minutes

Cook Time
30 minutes

Makes
12–14 servings

INGREDIENTS

2 litres (3¹/₂ pints) home-made beef or chicken stock

6 small or 4 medium beetroots, peeled and quartered

4 carrots, cut into thirds

1 onion, roughly chopped

2 garlic cloves, crushed

6–8 tbsp animal fat or coconut oil

1 tbsp sea salt

METHOD

1 In a large stockpot, combine the stock, beetroot, carrots, onion, garlic, and 2 or 3 tablespoons of animal fat. Bring to the boil over a medium-high heat.

2 Add the sea salt, lower the heat to medium-low, and simmer for 20 minutes.

3 Working in small batches, blend the soup in a blender (or use a hand-held blender) until smooth. For a thicker soup, simmer again for up to 10 more minutes.

4 Ladle into bowls, add 1 or 2 teaspoons of remaining animal fat to each portion, and serve.

" Occasionally, the blended carrot will begin to separate from the soup and form a bright orange foam. This is normal; just stir it back together. "

DAIRY FREE **NUT FREE**

Chicken Vegetable Soup

When it comes to vegetables, the more the better, and this warm, hearty, intro soup is packed with them. It's also a great dish for using up stock chicken.

Prep Time
15 minutes

Cook Time
25 minutes

Makes
4 servings

INGREDIENTS

- 1 litre (1³/₄ pints) home-made chicken stock
- 250g (8¹/₂oz) cooked shredded chicken (from stock, or poached leftovers)
- 100g (3¹/₂oz) carrots, chopped into 1.25cm (¹/₂in) pieces
- 120g (4oz) red onion, cut into 1.25cm (¹/₂in) pieces
- 4 garlic cloves, thinly sliced
- 100g (3¹/₂oz) yellow pepper, ribs and seeds removed, cut into 1.25cm (¹/₂in) pieces
- 60g (2oz) broccoli, stem removed, cut into 1.25cm (¹/₂in) florets
- 100g (3¹/₂oz) cauliflower, stem and core removed, cut into 1.25cm (¹/₂in) florets
- 180g (6oz) tomatoes, cored and diced into 1.25cm (¹/₂in) pieces
- 1 tbsp sea salt

METHOD

1 In a medium stockpot, combine the stock, chicken, carrots, red onion, garlic, yellow pepper, broccoli, cauliflower, tomatoes, and sea salt. Place over a medium-high heat and bring to the boil.

2 Reduce the heat to medium-low and simmer for 25 minutes or until the vegetables are tender.

3 If not serving immediately, place the pot in the sink and surround with cold water and ice cubes to cool the soup quickly.

4 Keep tightly covered in the fridge for up to 1 week, or freeze for up to 6 months.

Q&A

How do I freeze extra soup?

Doubling or tripling a soup recipe can save you time and effort later if you freeze some of the extra soup in individual portions. To freeze soup, be sure it's completely cool first. Place the cooled soup in containers or sealable plastic freezer bags, leaving about 2.5–5cm (1–2in) space at the top to allow for expansion. Label and date the containers, and freeze for up to 6 months.

Red onions

DAIRY FREE **NUT FREE** **PALEO DIET**

Garlicky Greens Soup

The slight bitterness of dark, leafy greens balances the sweetness of cooked garlic in this soup. If fresh greens aren't available, use thawed frozen spinach instead.

Prep Time
10 minutes

Cook Time
15 minutes

Makes
4 servings

INGREDIENTS

75g (2¹/₂oz) baby spinach leaves, roughly chopped

100g (3¹/₂ oz) Swiss chard leaves, tough stems removed, and chopped

75g (2¹/₂oz) dandelion leaves or wild rocket, roughly chopped

115g (4oz) lettuce leaves, chopped

75g (2¹/₂oz) watercress leaves, chopped

1 onion, diced

8 garlic cloves, thinly sliced

1.2 litres (2 pints) home-made chicken broth

2 tsp lemon juice

1 tbsp sea salt

METHOD

1 In a medium stockpot, combine the baby spinach, Swiss chard, dandelion greens or rocket, lettuce leaves, watercress, onion, garlic, and chicken broth. Place over a high heat and bring to the boil.

2 Reduce the heat to medium-low and simmer, uncovered, for 10 minutes, or until the leaves are softened.

3 Add lemon juice and sea salt, and stir into the soup until combined.

4 If not serving immediately, place the pot in the sink and surround with cold water and ice cubes to cool the soup quickly.

5 Store in the fridge tightly covered for up to 1 week, or freeze for up to 6 months.

Baby spinach

DAIRY FREE

NUT FREE

PALEO DIET

Sweet-and-Sour Chicken Vegetable Soup

Earthy Asian vegetables star in this fragrant, brothy soup that's ideal for using up stock chicken. Now chicken soup's not only good for the soul, it's great for the gut too.

Prep Time
15 minutes

Cook Time
20 minutes

Makes
4 servings

INGREDIENTS

- 1 litre (1 3/4 pints) home-made chicken stock
- 250g (8 1/2oz) cooked chicken (left over from making stock)
- 2 garlic cloves, sliced
- 2 tsp grated fresh root ginger
- 1 spring onion, chopped
- 1 onion, chopped
- 1 red pepper, ribs and seeds removed, chopped
- 60g (2oz) shiitake mushrooms, caps only, thinly sliced
- 50g (1 3/4oz) broccoli florets, chopped
- 1 carrot, thinly sliced
- 1 tsp sea salt
- 2 tbsp raw honey
- 60ml (2fl oz) lemon juice or fermented vegetable juice

METHOD

1 In a medium stockpot, combine the stock, chicken, garlic, ginger, spring onion, onion, red pepper, shiitake mushrooms, broccoli, carrots, and sea salt. Place over a medium-high heat and bring to the boil.

2 Cover, reduce the heat to medium-low and simmer for 20 minutes, or until the vegetables are just softened.

3 Uncover and stir in the honey and lemon juice.

❝ If fresh shiitakes aren't available, substitute whole cremini or chestnut button mushrooms, thinly sliced. ❞

Variation

Sweet-and-Sour Beef Vegetable Soup

Substitute 1 litre
($1^3/_4$ pints) beef stock
and 250g ($8^1/_2$oz)
cooked beef shank
(from making stock) for
the chicken stock and cooked chicken.

STAGE 1

DAIRY FREE   **NUT FREE**   **PALEO DIET**

Summer Garden Soup

This fresh, hearty soup captures the variety of the summer growing season in a bowl. It's a melting pot of vegetable goodness.

Prep Time
10 minutes

Cook Time
30 minutes

Makes
5 servings

INGREDIENTS

1 litre (1¾ pints) home-made chicken stock

4 garlic cloves, chopped

1 onion, chopped

1 carrot, cut into 1.25cm (½in) slices

1 small yellow squash, such as yellow courgette or patty pan, cut into 1.25cm (½in) slices

1 small courgette, cut into 1.25cm (½in) slices

1 red pepper, ribs and seeds removed, chopped

2 tomatoes, chopped

75g (2½oz) green beans, cut into 2.5cm (1in) pieces

2 tsp fresh lemon juice

2 tsp sea salt

METHOD

1 In a medium stockpot, combine the stock, garlic, onion, carrot, yellow squash, courgette, red pepper, tomatoes, green beans, lemon juice, and sea salt. Place over a high heat and bring to the boil.

2 Reduce the heat to medium-low and simmer, uncovered, for 25 minutes, or until the vegetables are tender.

3 If not serving immediately, place the pot in the sink and surround with cold water and ice cubes to cool the soup quickly.

4 Keep in the fridge, tightly covered, for up to 1 week.

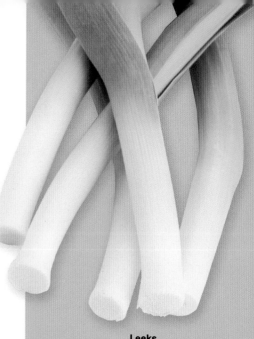

Leeks

Variation

Winter Garden Soup

STAGE 1

Use 4 chopped garlic cloves, 115g (4oz) chopped white part of leeks, 1 chopped carrot, 225g (8oz) cremini mushrooms, 1 peeled and diced turnip, 280g (9½oz) peeled and diced butternut squash, 2 teaspoons of lemon juice, 2 teaspoons of sea salt, and 1.2 litres (2 pints) of home-made chicken stock. Follow the main recipe as directed.

DAIRY FREE   **NUT FREE**   **PALEO DIET**

Three-Onion Soup

This onion, spring onion, and garlic soup has a deeply meaty flavour. In later stages, you can top it with a slice of toasted grain-free bread and grated Parmesan cheese, for a gut-healthy twist on the traditional French classic.

Prep Time
10 minutes

Cook Time
30 minutes

Makes
4 servings

INGREDIENTS

- 4 spring onions, thinly sliced on the diagonal
- 4 garlic cloves, thinly sliced
- 2 onions, halved and thinly sliced
- 1.4 litres (2½ pints) home-made beef stock
- 1 bay leaf
- 1 tbsp sea salt

METHOD

1 In a medium stockpot, combine the spring onions, garlic, onions, stock, bay leaf, and sea salt. Place over a high heat and bring to the boil.

2 Reduce the heat to medium-low, and simmer uncovered for 25 minutes. Remove the bay leaf.

3 If not serving immediately, place the pot in the sink and surround with cold water and ice cubes to cool the soup quickly.

4 Keep tightly covered in the fridge for up to 1 week.

Garlic

" If the onions, garlic, and spring onions aren't enough onion flavour for you, add 3 medium shallots, halved and thinly sliced. "

**NUT
FREE**

Pumpkin Bisque

Simple yet decadent, this soup features an often-overlooked nutritional star. A dollop of creamy, probiotic-rich home-made yogurt adds the finishing touch to a soup that's perfect for chilly weather.

Prep Time
10 minutes

Cook Time
20 minutes

Makes
4 servings

INGREDIENTS

2 small pumpkins, split, seeded, peeled, and cubed

1 onion, chopped

1 garlic clove, chopped

2 shiitake mushroom caps, chopped

1/2 tsp sea salt

1 tsp lemon juice

1.2 litres (2 pints) home-made chicken stock

4 tbsp home-made yogurt

2 tbsp ghee

METHOD

1 In a large stockpot, combine the pumpkins (or purée, see below), onion, garlic, mushrooms, salt, lemon juice, and stock. Place over a medium-high heat and bring to the boil.

2 Cover, reduce the heat to medium-low, and simmer for about 20 minutes, or until the pumpkin is softened.

3 Working in small batches, purée the soup in a blender, or use a hand-held blender.

4 Serve with a dollop of home-made yogurt and a drizzle of ghee.

“ When pumpkins aren't available, substitute one 425g can of organic pumpkin purée with no added ingredients. And if you can't find fresh shiitake mushrooms, use cremini or chestnut button mushrooms instead. **”**

Variation

Roasted Pumpkin Bisque

 STAGE 4

Substitute 675g (1½lb) roasted pumpkin purée for the pumpkins, and add 1 teaspoon of pumpkin pie spice. Cook and purée as directed, and garnish each serving with 1 tablespoon of home-made yogurt and 1 teaspoon of ghee.

Component

Roasted Pumpkin

STAGE 4

METHOD

1 Preheat the oven to 190°C (375°F/Gas 5). Lightly grease a baking tray with ghee.

2 Halve the pumpkin, place cut-side down on the prepared baking sheet, and roast for 30 minutes, or until tender when pierced with a knife.

3 Allow to cool, then scoop out and discard the seeds.

4 Scoop out and reserve the roasted pumpkin flesh. Discard the skin.

Roasted pumpkin

NUT FREE **PALEO DIET**

Creamy Tomato Soup

With a fresh, fruity taste and fragrance, this bright red soup is very versatile. Serve it warm during the cold months, or use your garden fresh tomatoes and serve it chilled when the weather is hot.

Prep Time
10 minutes

Cook Time
20 minutes

Makes
4 servings

INGREDIENTS

6 ripe tomatoes, chopped
1 onion, chopped
2 garlic cloves, chopped
1.2 litres (2 pints) home-made chicken stock
2 tsp sea salt
240ml (8fl oz) home-made yogurt (if tolerated)

METHOD

1 In a medium stockpot, combine the tomatoes, onion, garlic, chicken stock, and sea salt. Place over a high heat and bring to the boil.

2 Reduce the heat to medium-low, cover, and simmer for 15 minutes.

3 Remove from the heat, and purée the soup in small batches in a blender until smooth. Or use a hand-held blender.

4 If you can tolerate dairy, top each bowl with home-made yogurt before serving.

Tomatoes

" Puréeing hot soup can cause scalding burns. Fill the blender less than half full, cover with the lid but remove the centre knob, cover the lid and hole with a folded tea towel, and press down to secure. Blend. "

DAIRY FREE **NUT FREE** **PALEO DIET**

Greek Lemon Vegetable Soup

Lemon shines alongside a variety of hearty vegetables in this traditional Greek soup. Grated cauliflower floret "rice" provides the appeal of rice without the grain.

Prep Time
10 minutes

Cook Time
20 minutes

Makes
4 servings

INGREDIENTS

125g (4¹/₂oz) cooked chicken, shredded (from making stock)
3 garlic cloves, chopped
1 onion, diced
1 carrot, thinly sliced
¹/₂ tsp sea salt
1 litre (1³/₄ pints) home-made chicken stock
60ml (2fl oz) fresh lemon juice
2 tbsp ghee or animal fat
100g (3¹/₂oz) grated cauliflower florets
2 tomatoes, chopped
75g (2¹/₂oz) baby spinach, chopped
2 sprigs of flat-leaf parsley

METHOD

1 In a medium stockpot, combine the chicken, garlic, onion, carrot, sea salt, and chicken stock. Place over a medium-high heat and bring to the boil.

2 Reduce the heat to medium-low, cover, and cook for 20 minutes, or until the vegetables are softened. Remove from the heat.

3 Add the lemon juice and ghee.

4 Add the cauliflower, tomatoes, baby spinach, and flat-leaf parsley, and cook, stirring, for 3 minutes, until the vegetables are softened. Remove the parsley sprigs before serving.

Variation

Lemon Vegetable "Rice" Soup

STAGE 3

This is an easy, extra creamy variation.

1 Whisk 2 large free-range eggs in a medium bowl until frothy. Slowly whisk a ladle of the warm soup into the egg mixture. When combined, slowly whisk in another ladle of soup.

2 Transfer the egg mixture back into the soup pot, stirring frequently. Replace the parsley sprigs with 10g (¹/₄oz) chopped flat-leaf parsley, stirred into the soup after the egg mixture has been added.

Flat-leaf parsley

DAIRY FREE   NUT FREE   LOW FODMAP   PALEO DIET

Beetroot and Beef Short Rib Borscht

This vibrantly coloured soup is packed with flavourful vegetables and tender, juicy ribs. Even those who don't like beetroot will like this soup.

Prep Time
20 minutes

Cook Time
2 hours

Makes
6 servings

INGREDIENTS

2 bay leaves

1 bunch of fresh thyme

4 whole black peppercorns

4 bone-in short ribs, about 2kg (4lb) in total

1 tsp sea salt

2 garlic cloves, thinly sliced

325g (11oz) passata

1 litre (1³/₄ pints) home-made beef stock

1 onion, chopped into 1.25cm (¹/₂in) pieces

3 carrots, chopped into 1.25cm (¹/₂in) pieces

3 tomatoes, cored and chopped into 1.25cm (¹/₂in) pieces

4 beetroots, peeled and chopped into 1.25cm (¹/₂in) pieces

60ml (2fl oz) fermented vegetable juice

60ml (2fl oz) home-made yogurt (optional)

METHOD

1 Preheat the oven to 190°C (375°F/Gas 5). Bundle the bay leaves, thyme, and black peppercorns in a piece of cheesecloth, and tie it tightly closed.

2 Season the short ribs with sea salt, and place in a medium stockpot. Add the garlic, passata, beef stock, and cheesecloth bundle. Cover, and cook on the middle oven shelf for 1 hour.

3 Remove from the oven, and add the onion, carrots, tomatoes, and beetroot. Cover, return to the oven, and cook for 1 hour, or until the vegetables and meat are tender.

4 Remove from the oven, and remove and discard the cheesecloth bundle.

5 Pull the shredded beef from bones, and return to the pot. Fold in the fermented vegetable juice.

6 Garnish individual portions with yogurt (if using) and serve.

Beetroot

Variation

Slow-Cooker Beetroot and Beef Short Rib Borscht

STAGE 1

Increase the home-made beef stock to 1.4 litres (2½ pints) and combine the stock, ribs, sea salt, garlic, passata, onion, carrots, tomatoes, beetroot, and cheesecloth bundle in a 4-litre slow cooker. Cover and cook on a low setting for 8 hours. Transfer the cooked short ribs to a plate, and remove the beef from the bones. Return the meat to the cooker, and stir in the fermented vegetable juice. Remove and discard the cheesecloth bundle, garnish individual portions with yogurt (if using), and serve.

**NUT
FREE**

**LOW
FODMAP**

**PALEO
DIET**

Stewed Beef Porridge

The meat, fat, and connective tissue left over from making stock or bone broth is nourishing and easy on the gut. This recipe makes a quick breakfast that fills and fuels you, while saving money by using up leftovers.

Prep Time
5 minutes

Cook Time
10–12 minutes

Makes
1 serving

INGREDIENTS

140g (5oz) meat, fat, and connective tissue reserved from making broth or stock

120ml (4fl oz) home-made beef stock or broth

1–2 tsp animal fat, ghee, or coconut oil

sea salt

METHOD

1 In a blender, pulse the meat, fat, connective tissue, and beef stock until it reaches the desired consistency.

2 Transfer the purée to small saucepan, place over a medium heat, and cook for 5–7 minutes.

3 Add the animal fat, and cook for another 5 minutes, or until the fat has melted and combined.

4 Season with sea salt and serve immediately.

DAIRY FREE **NUT FREE**

Lemon Peppercorn Poached Chicken Breast

Infusing rich chicken stock with more aromatics produces a tangy, slightly peppery chicken dish. In later stages, add fresh ginger, sliced orange, star anise, coriander leaves, or even saffron to the poaching liquid.

Prep Time
10 minutes

Cook Time
20 minutes

Makes
4 servings

INGREDIENTS

4 sprigs of thyme
1 bay leaf
1 tsp whole black peppercorns
1 litre (1³/₄ pints) home-made chicken stock
60ml (2fl oz) fresh lemon juice
1 lemon, sliced
1 tsp sea salt
4 boneless, skinless chicken breasts

Lemon slices

METHOD

1 Bundle the thyme, bay leaf, and black peppercorns in a piece of cheesecloth, and tie tightly closed.

2 In a large, deep sauté pan, combine the chicken stock, lemon juice, lemon slices, cheesecloth bundle, and sea salt. Place over a high heat and bring to the boil.

3 Add the chicken breasts and cook for 3 minutes. Remove from the heat, cover, and set aside for 15 minutes.

4 Remove and discard the sliced lemon and the cheesecloth bundle.

5 If not using immediately, store the cooled chicken, tightly covered, in the fridge for up to 1 week.

" To reheat leftover poached chicken breasts, place them in a sauté pan over a medium-high heat with 60ml (2fl oz) chicken stock per breast. Bring to the boil, reduce the heat to medium-low, cover and simmer for 5 minutes, or until warmed through. "

DAIRY FREE

NUT FREE

PALEO DIET

Pan Steak with Mushrooms

Earthy mushrooms and tender sliced beef pair well with a side dish of creamy Cauliflower Mash. This is great for the meat-and-potato lover, or anyone looking for a hearty Stage 1 meal.

Prep Time
15 minutes

Cook Time
20 minutes

Makes
4 servings

INGREDIENTS

8 whole black peppercorns

1 sprig of thyme

1 skirt or top sirloin steak, about 450g (1lb)

1/2 tsp sea salt

2 garlic cloves, sliced

1 small onion, diced

45g (1 1/2oz) shiitake mushrooms, stems removed, halved

115g (4oz) chestnut button or cremini mushrooms

500ml (16fl oz) home-made beef stock

METHOD

1 Bundle the black peppercorns and thyme in a piece of cheesecloth, and tie tightly closed.

2 Season the steak on both sides with sea salt, and place in a large frying pan. Add the garlic, onion, shiitake mushrooms, button mushrooms, stock, and the cheesecloth bundle. Place over a medium-high heat and bring to the boil.

3 Cover, reduce the heat to medium-low, and simmer for 20 minutes, or until the internal temperature of the steak reaches 60°C (140°F) for medium.

4 Remove the steak from the pan, and allow to rest for 10 minutes. Cut into 4 pieces.

5 Remove and discard the cheesecloth bundle, and serve the steak with the sauce poured over.

Side Dish

Cauliflower Mash

You won't miss potatoes when you pair your steak with this healthy comfort dish, which you can make while the steak is cooking.

INGREDIENTS
1 head of cauliflower
½ tsp sea salt
60ml (2fl oz) ghee

METHOD
1 Core the cauliflower and cut into small florets. Place in a steamer basket in a large saucepan. Add 1.25cm (½in) water, place over a medium-high heat and bring to the boil. Cover, reduce the heat to medium-low, and simmer for 10 minutes or until the florets are tender.

2 Drain in a colander, pressing out any excess water. Place the cauliflower in a food processor fitted with a metal chopping blade, add sea salt and ghee, and process until smooth.

STAGE 1

STAGE 2

STAGE 3

STAGE 4

STAGE 2

STAGE 5

STAGE 6

FULL
DIET

DAIRY FREE

NUT FREE

PALEO DIET

Egg Drop Soup

Light, silky egg flowers complement the salty broth, meaty shiitake mushrooms, spring onions, and spicy ginger in this traditional Chinese super soup.

Prep Time
10 minutes

Cook Time
15 minutes

Makes
4 servings

INGREDIENTS

- 2 tbsp ghee or animal fat
- 1.4 litres (2½ pints) home-made chicken stock
- 115g (4oz) shiitake mushrooms, stems removed, sliced
- 100g (3½oz) spring onions, finely chopped
- 2 garlic cloves, crushed
- 1 tsp grated fresh root ginger
- 1 tbsp sea salt
- 6 large egg yolks, lightly beaten, or 3 large whole eggs, if yolks are tolerated well

METHOD

1 In a medium stockpot, combine the ghee, stock, shiitake mushrooms, spring onions, garlic, ginger, and salt. Place over a medium-high heat and bring to the boil.

2 Reduce the heat to medium-low and simmer, uncovered, for 15 minutes.

3 Remove from the heat and gently drizzle in the eggs, while stirring the broth slowly.

Shiitake mushrooms

" For a different flavour, you can substitute beef or fish stock. And if fresh shiitakes aren't available, substitute chestnut button or cremini mushrooms. "

DAIRY FREE **NUT FREE** **PALEO DIET**

Vegetable Beef Stewp

A cross between a soup and a stew, this bold one-pot dish features soft, chunky vegetables and mouthwatering, easy-to-digest beef – rich in protein and minerals – in a gravy-like broth.

Prep Time
15 minutes

Cook Time
45 minutes

Makes
4 servings

INGREDIENTS

450g (1lb) stewing beef

2 onions, chopped

2 carrots, chopped

180g (6oz) chopped tomatoes

1 garlic clove, finely chopped

1 bay leaf

3 sprigs of thyme, finely chopped

1 tbsp lemon juice

1 tsp sea salt

1 litre (1³/₄ pints) home-made beef stock

10g (¹/₄oz) flat-leaf parsley, chopped

METHOD

1 In a large stockpot, combine the beef, onions, carrots, tomatoes, garlic, bay leaf, thyme, lemon juice, and sea salt. Pour in the beef stock, place over a medium-high heat and bring to the boil.

2 Cover, reduce the heat to medium-low, and simmer for 45 minutes, or until the beef and vegetables are tender.

3 Stir in the flat-leaf parsley and remove the bay leaf. If the sauce isn't thick enough, uncover and continue to cook until it reaches your desired consistency.

Carrots

DAIRY FREE **NUT FREE** **PALEO DIET**

Braised Beef Burgers

These warm and juicy burgers, with onions, mushrooms, and tomatoes, feature a fragrant gravy – comfort food for a cold evening. You can serve them in a bowl topped with sauce, or on grain-free bread for a healthy version of the traditional burger. Either way, they're hearty and satisfying.

Prep Time
15 minutes

Cook Time
10 minutes

Makes
4 servings

INGREDIENTS

450g (1lb) minced beef

1 tsp sea salt

1 tbsp ghee, lard, or coconut oil

2 garlic cloves, chopped

225g (8oz) chestnut button mushrooms, sliced

1 small onion, diced

180g (6oz) diced tomatoes

240ml (8fl oz) home-made beef stock

1 tbsp thyme leaves, chopped

1 tbsp flat-leaf parsley, chopped

METHOD

1 Form the minced beef into four 2.5cm (1in) thick patties, and season evenly with sea salt.

2 Place the patties in a large frying pan. Add the ghee, garlic, mushrooms, onion, tomatoes, beef stock, thyme, and flat-leaf parsley. Place over a high heat and bring to the boil.

3 Cover, reduce the heat to medium-low, and cook for 10 minutes, or until the beef is cooked through and no pink remains in the centre of the patties.

4 Remove from the heat, and serve in a bowl, topped with sauce.

Variation

Mexicali Turkey Burgers

Substitute minced turkey for the beef and chicken stock for the beef stock. Omit the mushrooms, use red onion, and substitute 2 tablespoons of chopped coriander leaves for the thyme. Double the amount of chopped tomatoes, add 1 tablespoon of fresh lemon juice, and cook as directed for 15 minutes, or until no pink remains in the centre of the patties, and their internal temperature is 75°C (165°F). Top with 1 tablespoon of home-made yogurt. In stage 3, you can add $1/4$ of an avocado.

STAGE 2

DAIRY FREE

NUT FREE

PALEO DIET

Asian Braised Turkey Meatballs

These meatballs might not be exactly like your grandma's, but they're warm, juicy, and surrounded by satisfying flavours.

Prep Time
15 minutes

Cook Time
30 minutes

Makes
4 servings

INGREDIENTS

1kg (2lb) minced turkey thighs

4 large egg yolks

3 tsp sea salt

2 tbsp ghee or animal fat

1 litre (1³/₄ pints) home-made chicken stock

750g (1lb 10oz) passata

3 tbsp fresh lemon juice

1 tbsp grated fresh root ginger

4 garlic cloves, crushed

200g (7oz) spring onions, chopped

1 red onion, halved and sliced

1 red pepper, deseeded and sliced

1 yellow pepper, deseeded and sliced

1 carrot, sliced into 1.25cm (¹/₂in) rounds

10g (¹/₂oz) coriander leaves, chopped

METHOD

1 In a medium bowl, combine the turkey, egg yolks, and 1¹/₂ teaspoons of sea salt. Form the mixture into 32 equal balls.

2 In a medium casserole or stockpot, combine the ghee, chicken stock, passata, lemon juice, ginger, garlic, spring onions, red onion, red pepper, yellow pepper, carrot, coriander, and remaining 1¹/₂ teaspoons of sea salt. Place over a medium-high heat and bring to the boil.

3 Reduce the heat to medium-low, and gently add the meatballs to the pot one by one. Cover and cook for 30 minutes, or until the meatballs are cooked through and no pink remains.

Garlic

DAIRY FREE **NUT FREE** **PALEO DIET**

Chicken-Stuffed Cabbage Rolls

These little rolls are filled with warm and juicy chicken, wrapped in a softened cabbage shell, and covered with a tangy tomato broth.

Prep Time
30 minutes

Cook Time
30 minutes

Makes
4 servings

INGREDIENTS

1.8 litres (3¼ pints) water
8 large green cabbage leaves
1kg (2lb) minced chicken
1 large onion, chopped
4 garlic cloves, crushed
1 litre (1¾ pints) home-made chicken stock
150g (5½oz) grated cauliflower
2 tbsp ghee or animal fat
1kg (2¼lb) passata
2 bay leaves
1 tbsp sea salt

METHOD

1 In a medium stockpot, bring the water to the boil over a high heat. Reduce the heat to medium-low and add the cabbage, pressing the leaves down with a spoon. Cover, and cook for 10 minutes, or until soft. Remove the cabbage, drain, and set aside to cool.

2 In the pot, combine the chicken, onion, garlic, and half the chicken stock. Place over a medium-high heat and bring to the boil. Reduce the heat to medium-low, cover, and simmer for 15 minutes, or until the chicken is cooked. Stir in the cauliflower.

3 Place 1 softened cabbage leaf on a plate, curve side up with the stem towards you. Add ⅛ of the chicken mixture to the stem end. Fold the sides over about 2.5cm (1in), and roll up. Repeat with the remaining leaves and filling.

4 In a medium casserole or stockpot, combine the ghee, the remaining stock, passata, bay leaves, and sea salt. Add the cabbage rolls, seam-side down.

5 Place over a medium-high heat and bring to the boil. Reduce the heat to medium-low, cover, and simmer for 30 minutes. Remove the bay leaves and serve.

Green cabbage

DAIRY FREE   **NUT FREE**   **PALEO DIET**

Chicken Vegetable Ratatouille

Hearty and comforting, this colourful, vegetable-based stew is tasty cold or hot, depending on your preference. The Mediterranean influence captures the nourishing bounty of the summer season in one pot.

Prep Time
15 minutes

Cook Time
1 hour

Makes
4 servings

INGREDIENTS

4 skin-on, boned chicken leg quarters

1 tsp sea salt

1 litre (1³/₄ pints) home-made chicken stock

115g (4oz) diced onion

4 garlic cloves, sliced

115g (4oz) green pepper, ribs and seeds removed, diced

500g (1lb 2oz) aubergine, skin on, diced

175g (6oz) courgettes, diced

175g (6oz) yellow squash, such as yellow courgette or patty pan, diced

350g (12oz) diced tomatoes

10g (¹/₄oz) flat-leaf parsley, chopped

10g (¹/₄oz) basil leaves, chopped

60ml (2fl oz) ghee or animal fat

METHOD

1 Place the chicken leg quarters in a large, deep frying pan, and season with sea salt. Add chicken stock to cover about two-thirds of the chicken. Place over a medium-high heat.

2 When the stock begins to simmer, cover, reduce the heat to medium-low, and simmer for 45 minutes, or until the chicken legs are cooked through and have an internal temperature of 75°C (165°F).

3 Add the onion, garlic, green pepper, aubergine, courgette, yellow squash, and tomatoes. Cover and cook for 15 more minutes.

4 Remove from the heat. Add the flat-leaf parsley, basil, and ghee, and stir.

" Prevent food-borne illness by cooking chicken to an internal temperature of at least 75°C (165°F), as measured with a calibrated food thermometer. "

Variation

Winter Ratatouille

STAGE 2

In place of the ingredients in step 3, substitute the following:

4 garlic cloves, chopped

115g (4oz) chopped leeks, white part only

1 carrot, sliced into rounds

225g (8oz) halved cremini mushrooms

280g (9^1/$_2$oz) peeled, seeded, and diced butternut squash

350g (12oz) chopped tomatoes

2 tsp lemon juice

Increase the cooking time to 20 minutes, and continue with step 4.

DAIRY FREE

NUT FREE

PALEO DIET

Chicken Enchilada Casserole

This tasty Mexican one-pot is easy to assemble. Build flavour as you move through the diet by adding avocado in Stage 3 and ground cumin in Stage 5.

Prep Time
15 minutes

Cook Time
50 minutes

Makes
4 servings

INGREDIENTS

1 litre (1³/₄ pints)
   home-made
   chicken stock
500g (1lb 2oz) passata
180g (6oz) tomatoes,
   chopped
1 large red pepper, ribs
   and seeds removed,
   chopped
2 garlic cloves, chopped
1 large red onion,
   chopped
100g (3¹/₂oz) spring
   onions, chopped
120ml (4fl oz) lime juice
10g (¹/₄oz) chopped
   coriander leaves
2 tsp sea salt
8 bone-in, skin-on
   chicken thighs, about
   1.5kg (3lb) in total
240ml (8fl oz) home-
   made yogurt
   (optional)

METHOD

1 In a medium flameproof casserole, combine the chicken stock, passata, tomatoes, red pepper, garlic, red onion, spring onions, lime juice, coriander, and sea salt.

2 Add the chicken thighs on top of vegetables, so the chicken skin is just visible on the top of the broth. Place over a medium-high heat and bring to the boil.

3 Reduce the heat to medium-low, cover, and cook for 30 minutes.

4 Preheat the oven to 180°C (350°F/Gas 4). Remove the lid from the casserole, transfer to the oven, and cook for 10 minutes.

5 Place under the grill for 5 minutes, or until the chicken skin is browned.

6 Serve with a dollop of home-made yogurt (if using) in each bowl.

Coriander

Variations

Avocado Enchiladas

STAGE 3

In Stage 3, you can add a dollop of guacamole to the topping too.

Spicy Chicken Enchilada Casserole

STAGE 5

In Stage 5, you can pump up the flavour by adding ground cumin in Step 1.

DAIRY FREE
NUT FREE
PALEO DIET

Lemon Rosemary Salmon

This simple recipe results in a moist, light fillet with the aromas of lemon and rosemary. Make extra, allow to cool, and use flaked in omelettes and salads.

Prep Time
10 minutes

Cook Time
10 minutes

Makes
4 servings

INGREDIENTS

1 tsp sea salt

1kg (2lb) wild salmon, with skin, cut into 4 fillets

2 sprigs of thyme

4 sprigs of rosemary

60ml (2fl oz) fresh lemon juice

1 lemon, sliced

4 garlic cloves, chopped

1/2 onion, thinly sliced

1.4 litres (2 1/2 pints) home-made fish or chicken stock

METHOD

1 Sprinkle sea salt evenly over the salmon.

2 In a frying pan large enough to hold the fillets in a single layer without touching, combine the thyme, rosemary, lemon juice, lemon slices, garlic, onion, and fish stock. Place over a medium-high heat and bring to the boil.

3 Reduce the heat to medium-low, add the salmon, cover, and cook for 5 minutes, or until the salmon is cooked through.

4 Divide the salmon among 4 bowls. Strain the stock into a large pan, and pour evenly over each piece.

5 If not serving immediately, allow the salmon to cool completely, remove from the stock, and store tightly covered in the fridge for up to 1 week. Strain the stock, and keep in the fridge for up to 1 week or freeze for up to 6 months.

Variation

Lemon and Rosemary Butter-Poached Salmon

STAGE 4

1 Replace the fish stock with 1 litre (1 3/4 pints) ghee.

2 In a large frying pan over a medium-low heat, cook the ghee, thyme, rosemary, lemon juice, lemon slices, garlic, and onion for about 8 minutes, or until small bubbles begin to appear.

3 Add the salmon, and cook for 15 minutes, or until the top is completely opaque and flakes with a fork. Remove the salmon from the ghee, and serve.

Rosemary

DAIRY FREE **NUT FREE** **PALEO DIET**

Braised Tomato Sage Turkey Legs

Turkey isn't just for Christmas: it can provide great gut-supporting meals at any time of year. This recipe for juicy turkey in a rich tomato sauce, bursting with earthy sage, provides comfort in every bite.

Prep Time
20 minutes

Cook Time
1¼ hours

Makes
4 servings

INGREDIENTS

2 turkey legs, about 2.25kg (5lb) in total

½ tsp sea salt

1 medium onion, chopped

4 garlic cloves, chopped

2 carrots, roughly chopped

2 celery sticks, roughly chopped

4 sprigs of thyme

6 sprigs of sage

2 bay leaves

750ml (1¼ pints) home-made chicken stock

500g (1lb 2oz) passata

METHOD

1 Preheat the oven to 160°C (325°F/Gas 3). Place the turkey legs in a large ovenproof frying pan, and sprinkle with sea salt.

2 Add the onion, garlic, carrots, celery, thyme, sage, bay leaves, chicken stock, and passata.

3 Cover and cook on the middle oven shelf for 1¼ hours, or until the turkey legs are cooked through and reach an internal temperature of 75°C (165°F).

4 Remove the bay leaves from the pan, and allow the turkey to rest for 10 minutes before serving.

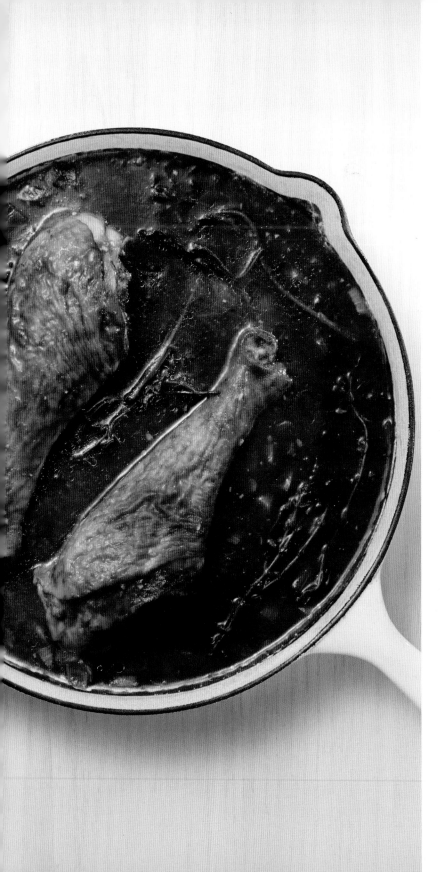

Bay leaves

Q&A

Can I make stock from the leftover turkey bones?

Yes you can! Follow the same steps and ingredients as in the Chicken Stock recipe, but reduce the water to 3 litres (4 ³/₄ pints). This makes about 2 litres (3 ¹/₄ pints) of turkey stock.

STAGE 1

STAGE 2

STAGE 3

STAGE 4

STAGE 3

STAGE 5

STAGE 6

FULL
DIET

DAIRY FREE **NUT FREE** **PALEO DIET**

Sauerkraut Scramble

Rich, warm eggs and tangy sauerkraut are perfectly matched in this fast and easy scramble. Any leftovers taste just as good cold too.

Prep Time
5 minutes

Cook Time
5 minutes

Makes
1 serving

INGREDIENTS

2 large eggs

2 tbsp water

$^1/_4$ tsp sea salt

1 tbsp ghee or animal fat

$^1/_2$ small red onion, finely chopped

1 garlic clove, crushed

75g (2½oz) Simple Sauerkraut

METHOD

1 In a small bowl, beat the eggs, water, and sea salt until blended and foamy.

2 Heat the ghee in a medium frying pan over a medium-high heat. When hot, add the onion and garlic, and cook, stirring, for about 2 minutes, or until soft. Add the Simple Sauerkraut, and stir to combine.

3 Pour the egg mixture into the middle of the pan. Using a spatula, gently push the cooked eggs from the edges of the pan towards the middle, so that the uncooked eggs can reach the hot surface.

4 Cook for about 2 minutes, gently moving the cooked egg until the entire surface has thickened and no liquid egg remains.

Eggs

NUT
FREE

PALEO
DIET

Santa Fe Breakfast Tostadas

This is a vibrant tower of delicious vegetables, tender chicken, and protein-rich eggs, topped with a rich avocado mash and tangy home-made yogurt.

Prep Time
15 minutes

Cook Time
7 minutes

Makes
2 servings

INGREDIENTS

4 large eggs

4 tbsp ghee or animal fat

125g (4^1/$_2$oz) cooked chicken, shredded

1 garlic clove, crushed

1 red onion, sliced

180g (6oz) chopped tomatoes

100g (3^1/$_2$oz) chopped spring onions

60g (2oz) sliced chestnut button mushrooms

1 carrot, coarsely grated

150g (5^1/$_2$oz) courgette, halved and sliced into 1.25cm (^{1}/$_2$in) half moons

150g (5^1/$_2$oz) yellow courgette, halved and sliced into 1.25cm (^{1}/$_2$in) half moons

1 tbsp chopped coriander leaves

^{1}/$_2$ tsp sea salt

115g (4oz) mashed avocado

120ml (4fl oz) yogurt (optional)

METHOD

1 In a small bowl, whisk the eggs until foamy. Heat a medium frying pan over a medium-high heat.

2 Add 2 tablespoons of ghee, the chicken, garlic, red onions, tomatoes, spring onions, button mushrooms, carrots, courgette, yellow courgette, coriander, and sea salt, and cook, stirring regularly, for 5 minutes, or until tender. Transfer to a plate and keep warm.

3 Add the remaining ghee to the pan, and pour the egg mixture into the centre. Using a spatula, gently push the cooked parts of the eggs from the edges towards the middle, so the uncooked eggs can reach the hot surface.

4 Cook for about 2 minutes, gently moving the cooked egg, until the entire surface has thickened and no liquid egg remains.

5 Divide the vegetables between 2 serving plates or bowls. Top each serving with half the scrambled eggs, half the avocado, and half the yogurt (if using).

DAIRY FREE **NUT FREE** **PALEO DIET**

Asparagus Fried Eggs

What better way to greet the day than with warm, protein-rich fried eggs and buttery, tender-crisp asparagus spears? Even on an elimination diet, breakfast can be the most important meal of the day.

Prep Time
5 minutes

Cook Time
5 minutes

Makes
2 servings

INGREDIENTS

12 asparagus spears, tough ends trimmed

60ml (2fl oz) home-made chicken stock

2 tbsp ghee or animal fat

2 tbsp chopped basil, coriander, mint, or flat-leaf parsley

4 large free-range eggs

1/4 tsp sea salt

METHOD

1 Place the asparagus spears in an even layer in a medium frying pan. Add the chicken stock and ghee, and sprinkle with the herbs. Place over a medium heat.

2 Crack 2 eggs over 6 asparagus spears and crack the remaining 2 eggs over the other 6 spears. Sprinkle the sea salt evenly over the eggs.

3 When the stock begins to boil, cover, reduce the heat to medium-low, and cook for 5 minutes, or until the egg whites have hardened and the asparagus is just softened.

Variation

Grilled Steak and Asparagus with Poached Eggs

INGREDIENTS

1 tsp ghee

½ tsp sea salt

12 asparagus spears

two 170g (6oz) skirt or
   top sirloin steaks

500ml (16fl oz) home-made
   chicken stock

4 large eggs

STAGE 4

METHOD

1 Preheat the grill to medium.
Spread ¹/₂ teaspoon ghee and
¹/₄ teaspoon sea salt on the
asparagus, and cover both sides
of the steaks with the remaining
ghee and sea salt.

2 Grill the steaks for 4 minutes each
side, rotating 90 degrees halfway
through. Turn the steaks and repeat.
Add the asparagus spears to the
grill when you turn the steaks,
turning them occasionally to cook
evenly. Transfer everything to a
plate, and let it rest for 10 minutes.

3 In a medium saucepan over a
medium-high heat, bring the stock
to the boil. Reduce the heat to
medium-low, gently crack the eggs
into the stock, and simmer for 3
minutes, until the whites are firm.

4 Divide the steak, asparagus, and
eggs between 2 plates. Season
with sea salt, and serve.

DAIRY
FREE

Roasted Butternut Squash Pancakes

These delicate, fluffy pancakes are a delight when served with sweet and nutty Almond Butter Honey Spread on top.

Prep Time
10 minutes

Cook Time
12 minutes

Makes
4 servings of
2 pancakes

INGREDIENTS

500g (1lb) roasted butternut squash purée, no skin or seeds

4 large egg yolks

$^3/_4$ tsp sea salt

120ml (4fl oz) ghee or animal fat

Almond Butter Honey Spread

METHOD

1 In a medium bowl, whisk together the roasted butternut, egg yolks, and sea salt.

2 Heat a large frying pan over a medium-low heat. Add half the ghee, and swirl the pan to distribute.

3 Using a tablespoon, add the butternut mixture to the pan, working in batches to avoid overcrowding. Gently press down on each pancake with a spatula to flatten to 5mm ($^1/_4$in) thickness. Cover, and cook the pancakes for 3 minutes.

4 Uncover, flip over the pancakes with a spatula, cover, and cook for another 3 minutes.

5 Transfer the cooked pancakes to a plate, and repeat with the remaining mixture and remaining ghee. Serve topped with Almond Butter Honey Spread.

Topping

Almond Butter Honey Spread

STAGE 3

To make this spread, whisk together 60g (2oz) all-natural almond butter and 4 teaspoons raw honey in a small bowl. Pour into a small pan, place over a medium heat, and cook, whisking constantly, for 3 minutes. When the ingredients are combined and warmed, reduce the heat to low.

Honey

DAIRY FREE **NUT FREE** **PALEO DIET**

Easy Avocado Omelette

A soft blanket of eggs with smooth, rich avocado tucked into the centre, this omelette works wonderfully for any meal.

Prep Time
5 minutes

Cook Time
5 minutes

Makes
1 serving

INGREDIENTS

2 large eggs
2 tbsp water
$^1/_4$ tsp sea salt
1 tbsp ghee or animal fat
$^1/_2$ small red onion, finely chopped
$^1/_2$ garlic clove, crushed
60g (2oz) mashed avocado

METHOD

1 In a small bowl, beat the eggs, water, and sea salt until blended and foamy.

2 Heat the ghee in a medium frying pan over a medium-high heat. When hot, add the red onion and garlic, and cook, stirring, for about 2 minutes.

3 Pour the egg mixture into the centre of the pan. Using a spatula, gently push the cooked eggs from the edges towards the middle of the pan, so the uncooked eggs can reach the hot surface. Cook for about 2 minutes, gently moving the cooked egg, until the surface has thickened and no liquid egg remains.

4 Place the avocado on one side of the cooked eggs, and use the spatula to fold the omelette over onto the avocado.

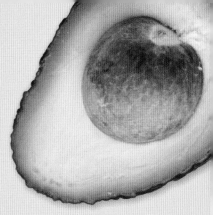

Avocado

Variation

Salmon, Spinach, and Tomato Omelette with Avocado

In addition to the ingredients in step 2, add 45g (1$^1/_2$oz) chopped tomato, 20g ($^3/_4$oz) chopped baby spinach, and 60g (2oz) cup poached and flaked salmon. After cooking for 2 minutes, add 1 teaspoon of fresh lemon juice and 2 teaspoons of chopped basil, and stir. Proceed with step 3.

STAGE 3

DAIRY FREE

NUT FREE

PALEO DIET

Aromatic Chicken with Mushrooms

Mushrooms, garlic, and onions complement the juicy chicken in this warm and filling dish. Serve with Simple Roasted Root Vegetables for a satisfying and gut-friendly meal.

Prep Time
15 minutes

Cook Time
30 minutes

Makes
4 servings

INGREDIENTS

2 onions, thinly sliced

450g (1lb) button, cremini, or baby portobello mushrooms, sliced

2 garlic cloves, finely chopped

2 tbsp coconut oil, ghee, or lard

4 chicken breasts, skin on, each about 170g (6oz)

sea salt

500ml–1 litre (³/₄–1³/₄ pints) home-made chicken stock

METHOD

1 Preheat the oven to 180°C (350°F/Gas 4).

2 In a large ceramic casserole dish, combine the onions, mushrooms, and garlic. Add the coconut oil, and place the chicken breasts on top. Sprinkle with sea salt, and fill the dish with chicken stock until just a bit of chicken skin is exposed.

3 Bake for 30 minutes, or until the skin is brown and slightly crispy.

4 To serve, top the chicken breasts with the mushrooms and onions.

Side Dish

Simple Roasted Root Vegetables

Chop 1 beetroot, 3 large carrots, and 2 turnips into 1.25cm (1/2in) dice. Toss with 2 tablespoons of melted coconut oil and 1/2 teaspoon of sea salt, and place in a baking dish. Roast at 200°C (400°F/Gas 6) for 45 minutes, stirring after 20 minutes. Makes 4 servings.

STAGE 1

STAGE 2

STAGE 3

STAGE 4

STAGE 4

STAGE 5

STAGE 6

FULL DIET

DAIRY FREE **PALEO DIET**

Ginger Pumpkin Muffins

The rich flavour of pumpkin spice is baked into this delicate, soft, and satisfying muffin that's great any time of year.

Ginger

Prep Time
15 minutes

Cook Time
25 minutes

Makes
12 muffins

INGREDIENTS

350g (12oz) almond flour
1/2 tsp baking soda
1/4 tsp sea salt
1 1/2 tsp ground cinnamon
1 1/2 tsp ground ginger
1/4 tsp ground nutmeg
30g (1oz) walnut pieces, soaked and dried
225g (8oz) canned, unsweetened pumpkin purée, or home-made roasted pumpkin/ butternut purée
60ml (2fl oz) raw honey
4 large free-range eggs
1/2 tsp pure vanilla extract

METHOD

1 Preheat the oven to 160°C (325°F/Gas 3). Oil the bottoms and sides of a non-stick 12-cup muffin tray with 1 teaspoon of coconut oil.

2 In a medium bowl, combine the almond flour, baking soda, sea salt, cinnamon, ginger, nutmeg, and walnuts.

3 In a separate medium bowl, whisk together the pumpkin purée, honey, eggs, and vanilla extract.

4 Pour the dry ingredients into the wet ingredients, and stir until well combined.

5 Fill each muffin cup equally with the mixture, and bake on the middle oven shelf for 25 minutes, or until a skewer inserted into the muffin comes out clean.

6 Cool the muffins for 15 minutes before serving. Remove from the tin using a rubber spatula if needed.

DAIRY FREE   **PALEO DIET**

Chicken Muffins

Cook a double or triple batch of these protein-packed muffins at the weekend, freeze them, and you'll have quick and easy meals or snacks to reheat and enjoy throughout the week.

Prep Time
20 minutes

Cook Time
35 minutes

Makes
6 muffins

INGREDIENTS

$1/2$ small onion, chopped

$1/2$ small green pepper, chopped

$1/2$ carrot, chopped

$1/4$ small yellow courgette, chopped

2 garlic cloves, crushed

675g ($1^1/_2$lb) minced chicken, preferably dark meat

$1/2$ tsp sea salt

$1/4$ tsp ground black pepper

$1/4$ tsp dried oregano

$1/4$ tsp dried basil

$1/4$ tsp dried rosemary

1 large egg

60g (2oz) almond flour

2 tbsp tomato purée

METHOD

1 Preheat the oven to 180°C (350°F/Gas 4). Lightly oil a 6-cup king-size (9 × 7.5cm) muffin tin with animal fat or coconut oil.

2 In a medium frying pan over a medium-high heat, sauté the onion, green pepper, carrot, yellow courgette, and garlic for 3–4 minutes, or until soft. Set aside to cool.

3 In a large bowl, using clean hands, combine the chicken, vegetables, sea salt, black pepper, oregano, basil, rosemary, egg, almond flour, and tomato purée.

4 Divide the mixture evenly among the muffin cups, and bake for 35 minutes.

5 Serve immediately, or freeze muffins individually.

Yellow courgettes

DAIRY
FREE

NUT
FREE

PALEO
DIET

Green Goddess Juice

This refreshing elixir is full of antioxidants, minerals, and compounds that supercharge the liver, help digestion, and reduce inflammation.

Prep Time
15 minutes

Makes
2 servings

INGREDIENTS

30g (1oz) baby spinach
75g (2¹⁄₂oz) kale, ends trimmed
60g (2oz) peeled, deseeded, and
    chopped cucumber
1 small green apple, cored
juice of ¹⁄₂ small lime
10g (¹⁄₄oz) coriander leaves
1 kiwi fruit, peeled
1 tbsp fresh root ginger

METHOD

1 Process the baby spinach, kale, cucumber, green apple, lime juice, coriander, kiwi fruit, and ginger in a juicer, or purée in a blender. If blending, strain into a small bowl by squeezing the pulp through four layers of cheesecloth.

2 Serve the juice immediately.

DAIRY
FREE

NUT
FREE

PALEO
DIET

Peppery Pear Juice

Peppery rocket is mellowed by the sweetness of pears in this tasty juice. Lemon adds a pop of citrus and helps cleanse the liver.

Prep Time
15 minutes

Makes
2 servings

INGREDIENTS

4 pears, cored and quartered
1 lemon, peeled, deseeded, white
    pith removed
4 large celery sticks
60g (2oz) rocket

METHOD

1 Process the pears, lemon, celery, and rocket in a juicer, or purée in a blender. If blending, strain into a small bowl by squeezing the pulp through four layers of cheesecloth.

2 Serve the juice immediately.

❝ These juices help keep the liver healthy so it can keep processing the high-quality fats you're consuming to heal your gut. ❞

DAIRY FREE NUT FREE PALEO DIET

Liver-Loving Juice

Beetroot and ginger pack a powerful punch. Beetroot helps your liver in producing bile to digest gut-healing high-quality fat. Ginger calms your stomach and helps boost your immune system.

Prep Time
15 minutes

Makes
2 servings

INGREDIENTS

- 1 piece fresh root ginger, about 3.75cm (1½in), peeled and chopped
- 4 large carrots, coarsely chopped
- 1 large beetroot, scrubbed and cut into 5cm (2in) chunks
- 1 red apple, such as Gala, cored and cut into 8

METHOD

1 Process the ginger, carrots, beetroot, and apple in a juicer, or purée in a blender. If blending, strain into a small bowl by squeezing the pulp through four layers of cheesecloth.

2 Serve the juice immediately.

Variation

Golden Goddess Juice

Replace the apple with an orange, peeled, deseeded, and white pith removed. Reduce the carrots to 2, and add 115g (4oz) spinach.

STAGE 4

DAIRY FREE **NUT FREE** **PALEO DIET**

Garlic Chicken with Vegetables

Buttery-sweet, garlic-crisped skin accompanies delicious, tender meat in this one-pot dish. The juices from the chicken help create tender caramelized, vegetables. You can easily substitute these, according to your stage.

Prep Time
15 minutes

Cook Time
1 hour

Makes
4 servings

INGREDIENTS

- 1½ medium onions, halved and then quartered
- 2 carrots, cut into 2.5cm (1in) rounds
- 100g (3½oz) celery, cut into 5cm (2in) pieces
- 140g (5oz) green beans, ends trimmed, and halved crosswise
- 3 tbsp ghee or animal fat
- 2 tsp rosemary
- 3 tsp sea salt
- 8 chicken thighs, skin-on, about 1.5kg (3lb) in total
- 4 garlic cloves
- 2 tbsp chopped thyme

METHOD

1 Preheat the oven to 200°C (400°F/ Gas 6).

2 In a large bowl, combine the vegetables, 1 tablespoon of ghee, the rosemary, and 1 teaspoon of sea salt. Transfer to an ovenproof glass baking dish, and spread in an even layer.

3 In the same bowl, toss together the chicken, the remaining 2 teaspoons of sea salt, the garlic, thyme, and remaining 2 tablespoons of ghee.

4 Evenly distribute the chicken on top of the vegetables in the dish. Bake on the middle shelf for 1 hour, or until the chicken reaches 75°C (165°F).

Q&A

What's the best way to store herbs?

Herbs are often sold in larger bunches than you need for a recipe. Rather than throwing away the extra herbs, or letting them go bad before you're able to use them, you can easily store them for later use. For delicate herbs like flat-leaf parsley, basil, and mint, trim off the ends and discard any browned leaves. Add 2.5cm (1in) water to a glass jar, place the herbs trimmed side down in the jar, cover with the lid or a plastic bag, and store in the fridge. For hardier herbs like thyme and rosemary, place the herbs in a single layer on moist kitchen paper, roll them up, and store in a sealed plastic bag in the fridge. Change the kitchen paper or jar water once a week.

Rosemary

PALEO DIET **LOW FODMAP**

Grilled Salmon with Walnut Pesto

The perfect balance of fresh herbs and zesty lemon brings a wonderful brightness to slightly smoky, omega-3-rich grilled salmon.

Prep Time
10 minutes

Cook Time
10 minutes

Makes
4 servings plus extra pesto

INGREDIENTS

$^1/_2$ tsp sea salt

3 garlic cloves

115g (4oz) walnuts, soaked and dried

60g (2oz) flat-leaf parsley

2 tbsp fresh chives

2 tbsp coriander leaves

2 tbsp basil leaves

3 tsp grated lemon zest

120ml (4fl oz) extra virgin olive oil

675g (1$^1/_2$lb) wild salmon, cut into four fillets of about 175g (6oz)

METHOD

1 Preheat the grill on a medium setting.

2 In a food processor fitted with a metal chopping blade, process the sea salt, garlic, walnuts, flat-leaf parsley, chives, coriander, basil, lemon zest, and olive oil until smooth.

3 Place the salmon skin-side up on the grill, cover, and cook for 5 minutes, rotating the fish 90 degrees halfway through the cooking time.

4 Turn the fish, spread 2 tablespoons of pesto on the grilled side of each fillet and cook for another 5 minutes, rotating the fish 90 degrees halfway through the cooking time.

Q&A

What can I do with leftover pesto?

You'll have a good cupful of leftover pesto with this recipe. You can use it as a condiment for grilled chicken or roast beef, mix it in with scrambled eggs, or serve it as a dip for vegetables. Or for a quick and easy bruschetta, spread some pesto on a piece of toasted Everyday Grain-Free Bread, and top with chopped tomatoes and a little sea salt. Just remember to store the extra pesto tightly covered in the fridge until ready to use.

Basil

DAIRY FREE **NUT FREE** **PALEO DIET**

"Spaghetti" with Pomodoro Sauce

Long, delicate courgette spaghetti will curb any pasta craving – especially when paired with your choice of sauce. This recipe is for a light tomato and basil sauce, but the options are endless.

Prep Time
15 minutes

Cook Time
5 minutes

Makes
2 servings

INGREDIENTS

2 courgettes, ends trimmed
275g (9oz) diced tomatoes
20g (³/₄oz) chopped basil leaves
1 garlic clove, chopped
¹/₄ tsp sea salt
¹/₄ tsp black pepper
2 tbsp ghee

METHOD

1 Lay a box grater flat on your worktop, with the largest holes face up. Push the courgette lengthways across the top of the grater, rotate it, and push across the grater again. Repeat until the whole courgette is shredded into noodles. (Alternatively, use a vegetable spiralizer or mandoline.)

2 In a medium bowl, combine the tomatoes, basil, garlic, sea salt, and black pepper.

3 In a medium frying pan, heat the ghee over a medium heat. Add the courgette spaghetti, and cook, stirring occasionally, for 3¹/₂ minutes, or until just softened.

4 Add the sauce to the courgettes, and cook, stirring, for about 1¹/₂ minutes, until the sauce has warmed and completely coats the spaghetti.

Variations

Tahini Lemon Sauce

STAGE 4

In a food processor or blender, process 4 spring onions, 15g ($1/2$oz) coriander leaves, 1 tablespoon of crushed dried chillies (optional), 2 teaspoons of sesame seeds, 100g ($31/2$oz) tahini, 60ml (2fl oz) lemon juice, 2 teaspoons of sesame oil, 1 teaspoon of honey, 60ml (2fl oz) stock, $1/2$ teaspoon of sea salt, and $1/4$ teaspoon of black pepper until smooth.

Spinach Pesto Sauce

FULL DIET

In a food processor or blender, process 60g (2oz) soaked and dried walnuts, 60g (2oz) flat-leaf parsley, 75g ($21/2$oz) baby spinach, 2 garlic cloves, 20g ($3/4$oz) chives, $1/4$ teaspoon of sea salt, and $1/4$ teaspoon of black pepper. On a low speed, slowly drizzle in 180ml (6fl oz) extra virgin olive oil. When combined, stir in 50g ($13/4$oz) grated Parmesan cheese.

DAIRY FREE **PALEO DIET**

Oven-Roasted Turkey Meatloaf

This fresh and filling meatloaf is juicy and delicious — and the vegetables are cooked right in. For a quick meal, place a slice of leftover meatloaf between two slices of Everyday Grain-Free Bread.

Prep Time
15 minutes

Cook Time
1 hour

Makes
8 servings

INGREDIENTS

- 120g (4oz) onion, finely chopped
- 250g (9oz) passata
- 2 tbsp raw honey
- 900g (2lb) minced turkey
- 2 large eggs, beaten
- 60g (2oz) ground almonds
- 150g (5$^1/_2$oz) chopped frozen spinach, thawed, squeezed, and drained
- 2 garlic cloves, crushed
- 50g (1$^3/_4$oz) spring onions, green part only, finely chopped
- 1 small red pepper, ribs and seeds removed, finely chopped
- 1 carrot, grated
- 30g (1oz) shiitake mushroom caps, sliced
- 1 tsp sea salt

METHOD

1 Preheat the oven to 180°C (350°F/Gas 4). In a small bowl, whisk one-third of the onion together with the passata and the honey.

2 In a medium bowl, combine the turkey, eggs, ground almonds, remaining onion, spinach, garlic, spring onions, red pepper, carrot, shiitake mushrooms, and sea salt. Transfer the mixture to a 23 × 33cm (9 × 13in) ovenproof baking dish, and using your hands, form into a loaf that measures about 15 × 7.5cm (6 × 3in).

3 Pour the tomato mixture over the meatloaf, and spread evenly over the sides and top.

4 Bake on the middle shelf for 1 hour, or until the internal temperature reaches 70°C (160°F). Cool the meatloaf for 10 minutes before slicing and serving.

" If you're not keen on turkey, substitute minced chicken or beef, and prepare in the same way. Or combine equal portions of chicken, turkey, and beef. "

DAIRY FREE

NUT FREE

PALEO DIET

Classic Pot Roast with Onions

Lightly seasoned beef is slowly roasted in its own juices with hearty garlic and onions and aromatic rosemary and thyme.

Prep Time
15 minutes

Cook Time
4 hours

Makes
8 servings

INGREDIENTS

$^1/_2$ tsp sea salt

2kg (4lb) braising steak

2 tbsp ghee or animal fat

4 onions, quartered

4 carrots, cut into 5cm (2in) pieces

4 garlic cloves, halved

3 sprigs of rosemary

5 sprigs of thyme

750ml (1$^1/_4$ pints) home-made beef stock

METHOD

1 Preheat the oven to 140°C (275°F/ Gas 1). Spread the sea salt evenly over all sides of the beef.

2 In a large stockpot or flameproof casserole, heat 1 tablespoon of ghee over a medium heat. Add the onions, carrots, garlic, rosemary, and thyme, and sauté, stirring, for 4 minutes, or until lightly browned. Carefully transfer to a plate.

3 Add the remaining ghee to the pot, return the meat, and sear for 1 minute per side or until browned. Remove from the heat and transfer the meat to a plate.

4 Return the vegetables and herbs to the pot, place the meat on top, and add the beef stock. Cover, and cook on the middle oven shelf for 4 hours, or until tender.

Onions

Variation

Slow-Cooker Pot Roast with Onions

STAGE 4

Omit the fat, and combine the sea salt, carrots, garlic, onions, rosemary and thyme (tied with butcher's twine or cheesecloth for easy removal), and beef stock in a slow cooker. Add the beef, cover, and cook at a low setting for 8 hours. Carefully remove the beef, and allow it to sit for 5 minutes before slicing it against the grain.

NUT FREE

Minced Beef Stroganoff

Tender beef and mushrooms are paired with a tangy, home-made yogurt sauce. Deliciously simple, this quick recipe is sure to become your go-to meal on busy weeknights, especially when served with Butternut Squash Gnocchi.

Prep Time
10 minutes

Cook Time
25 minutes

Makes
4 servings

INGREDIENTS

450g (1lb) minced beef
225g (8oz) chestnut button mushrooms, sliced
1 large onion, chopped
3 garlic cloves, chopped
300ml (10fl oz) home-made beef stock
1/2 tsp sea salt
1 tsp chopped rosemary
10g (1/4oz) chopped parsley
240ml (8fl oz) home-made yogurt
60ml (2fl oz) ghee or animal fat

METHOD

1 In a large frying pan, combine the mince, button mushrooms, onion, garlic, beef stock, and sea salt. Place over a medium-high heat and bring to the boil.

2 Cover, reduce the heat to medium-low, and cook for 20 minutes. Remove from the heat.

3 Stir in the rosemary and parsley. Serve topped with a dollop of yogurt and a drizzle of ghee.

Side Dish

Butternut
Squash
Gnocchi

FULL
DIET

INGREDIENTS

1 large egg

225g (8oz) mashed butternut
  squash

175g (6oz) almond flour

30g (1oz) coconut flour

25g (1oz) grated Parmesan
  cheese

1½ tsp sea salt

½ tsp black pepper

¼ tsp ground nutmeg

METHOD

1 In a medium bowl, gently whisk
the egg until the yolk and white are
combined. Add the butternut squash,
almond flour, coconut flour, Parmesan
cheese, sea salt, black pepper, and
nutmeg, and mix well.

2 Form the dough into a tight mound.
Scoop out 1 tablespoon, roll between
your palms to form a small ball, and
squeeze gently between your thumb
and index finger to form a cylinder.
Gently drag the tines of a fork
over the top. Repeat to use up all
the mixture.

3 Fill a medium saucepan with water
to a depth of 5cm (2in), place over a
medium-high heat, bring to the boil,
and reduce the heat to a simmer.

4 Add 10 gnocchi at a time, and cook
for 2 minutes. Using a slotted spoon,
transfer the gnocchi to a plate to
drain, and then repeat with the
remaining gnocchi.

DAIRY FREE

PALEO DIET

Minced Beef Empanadas

The nuttiness of almond flour, citrus-toned coriander, and tangy lime combine to give these savoury stuffed and baked pastries an exotic flavour. And they're just the right size for an afternoon snack.

Prep Time
15 minutes

Cook Time
30 minutes

Makes
7 servings of 2 empanadas

INGREDIENTS

450g (1lb) almond flour

4 large free-range eggs

8 tbsp coconut oil, melted over a low heat

3 tsp sea salt

3 tbsp ghee or animal fat

680g (1$\frac{1}{2}$lb) minced beef

6 garlic cloves, crushed

225g (8oz) onion, finely chopped

400g (14oz) tomatoes, finely chopped

85g (3oz) passata

75ml (3$\frac{1}{2}$oz) beef stock

20g ($\frac{3}{4}$oz) coriander leaves

1 tbsp lime juice

METHOD

1 Preheat the oven to 180°C (350°F/Gas 4). Line a baking sheet with baking parchment.

2 In a medium bowl, combine the almond flour, eggs, coconut oil, and 1$\frac{1}{2}$ teaspoons of sea salt. Form and press the dough into a mound, wrap in cling film, and store in the fridge until needed.

3 In a medium frying pan over a medium heat, combine the ghee, minced beef, garlic, remaining sea salt, and onion, and cook for 5 minutes, stirring and breaking up the larger chunks.

4 Add the tomatoes, passata, and beef stock, and cook for 10 minutes or until the beef is fully cooked and the liquid mostly reduced. Stir in the coriander and lime juice, and set aside to cool completely.

5 Divide the dough into 14 small mounds. Place a 15 × 15cm (6 × 6in) piece of baking parchment or cling film on your worktop. Place a dough ball on the paper, and flatten it to a circle 12.5cm (5in) in diameter. Place 3 tablespoons of the cooled beef mixture on half of dough circle, carefully lift the opposite side of the paper, fold it over to enclose the filling, and press gently to seal. (Note that the dough doesn't contain gluten so it won't be stretchy.) Repeat with the remaining dough and beef mixture.

6 Gently place the empanadas on the baking sheet using a spatula. Bake on the middle oven shelf for 20 minutes, or until the dough is browned and the filling warmed.

DAIRY FREE

PALEO DIET

Crackling Nuts

Nuts contain phytic acid, which binds to minerals during digestion and prevents the body from properly absorbing them. Soaking nuts in saltwater neutralizes the acid, making the nuts easier to digest.

Prep Time
5 minutes
+ 7 hours

Cook Time
12–24 hours

Makes
16 servings

INGREDIENTS

450g (1lb) pecans, walnuts, pine nuts, macadamia nuts, hazelnuts, or cashews

warm spring or filtered water

1 tbsp sea salt

METHOD

1 Place the nuts in a medium bowl, add warm spring water to cover, season with sea salt, and stir to combine. Set aside at room temperature for 7 hours.

2 Strain the nuts through a fine sieve, and rinse. Spread them in an even layer on a baking sheet and bake for 12–24 hours at no more than 65°C (150°F). (Or use a dehydrator.)

3 Store the nuts in an airtight container in the fridge for up to 3 months, or freeze for up to 6 months.

Variation

Crackling Seeds

STAGE 4

Swap out the nuts for your favourite seeds. Seeds such as sunflower and pumpkin seeds also contain phytic acid, and should be soaked and dried in the same way as the nuts.

STAGE 1

STAGE 2

STAGE 3

STAGE 4

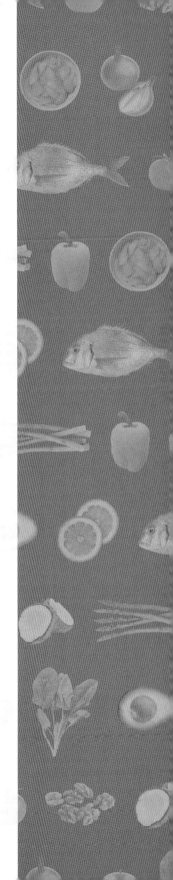

STAGE 5

STAGE 5

STAGE 6

FULL
DIET

DAIRY FREE   NUT FREE   LOW FODMAP   PALEO DIET

Simple House Salad

Now that you can tolerate raw vegetables, you can easily increase your intake with this quick combination of tender leaves and refreshing cucumber in a tangy, fruity vinaigrette.

Prep Time
10 minutes

Makes
2 servings

INGREDIENTS

1 tbsp fresh lemon juice

3 tbsp extra virgin olive oil

$^1/_2$ tsp sea salt

225g (8oz) butterhead lettuce, soft leaves, chopped

115g (4oz) cucumber, peeled, deseeded, and sliced into thin rounds

METHOD

1 In a small bowl, whisk together the lemon juice, olive oil, and sea salt.

2 Place the lettuce and cucumber in a medium bowl, pour the lemon vinaigrette over, and toss to coat.

Variation

Garden Salad

STAGE 5

Add 1 grated carrot, 85g (3oz) chopped or sliced tomato, and 1 slice of red onion. In Stage 6, you can incorporate 75g (2$^1/_2$oz) raw fruit, such as apples, berries, cherries, or grapes.

Butterhead lettuce

" In addition to soft butterhead lettuce, Lollo Rosso, baby spinach, and cos work well in this recipe. "

DAIRY FREE **NUT FREE** **PALEO DIET**

Grain-Free Tabbouleh

In this updated version of the traditional Lebanese salad, cauliflower is substituted for the usual bulgur wheat for an interesting, healthy variation, while parsley adds beneficial minerals and antioxidants.

Prep Time	**Makes**	**Makes**
20 minutes	5 minutes	24–30 servings

INGREDIENTS

$^1/_2$ head of cauliflower, florets only, chopped extremely finely with a knife or in a food processor

175g (6oz) flat-leaf parsley, finely chopped

10g ($^1/_4$oz) mint, finely chopped

2 tomatoes, chopped into 5mm ($^1/_4$in) dice

$^1/_2$ cucumber, peeled, deseeded, and chopped into 5mm ($^1/_4$in) dice

3 tbsp olive oil

3 tbsp fresh lemon juice

$^3/_4$ tsp sea salt

$^1/_4$ tsp black pepper

METHOD

1 In a small saucepan, bring 750ml (1$^1/_4$ pints) of water to the boil over a high heat. Reduce the heat to medium-low, add the cauliflower, and cook for 5 minutes.

2 Drain the cauliflower in a fine sieve and transfer to a medium bowl.

3 Add the flat-leaf parsley, mint, tomatoes, cucumber, olive oil, lemon juice, sea salt, and black pepper, and mix well until combined. Serve immediately, or store tightly covered in the fridge for up to 1 week.

" After Stage 2, consider roasting the cauliflower instead of boiling it. Toss finely diced or processed cauliflower with coconut oil or animal fat, season with 1 teaspoon of sea salt, and roast on a baking sheet at 220°C (425°F/Gas 7) for 25–40 minutes, depending on how brown and crispy you want it. "

DAIRY FREE **NUT FREE**

Mini Butternut Squash Soufflés

Light, fluffy, and subtly sweet, these easy butternut squash soufflés are a great option for weekend brunches.

Prep Time
10 minutes

Cook Time
30 minutes

Makes
6 servings

INGREDIENTS

12 large free-range eggs
350g (12oz) butternut squash purée
1 tsp sea salt
Raw honey (optional)

METHOD

1 Preheat the oven to 180°C (350°F/Gas 4). Grease six 500ml (16fl oz) soufflé dishes or 12 250ml (8fl oz) ramekins with coconut oil or ghee.

2 In a medium bowl, beat the eggs. Add the butternut squash purée and sea salt, mix well, and pour into the prepared ramekins.

3 Bake for 30 minutes, or until the soufflés have puffed up and a skewer or knife inserted into the centre comes out clean.

4 Drizzle the soufflés with raw honey (if using), and serve.

Component

Butternut Squash Purée

To make your own butternut squash purée, follow these steps:

1 Preheat the oven to 200°C (400°F/Gas 6). Cut 1 butternut squash in half and scoop out the seeds.

2 Place on a baking sheet, and roast for 45 minutes, or until soft and easily pierced with a fork.

3 Scoop the squash into a blender or a food processor fitted with a metal chopping blade, and process until smooth. (You might need to do this in batches.)

4 Store in the fridge for up to 1 week.

Butternut squash

DAIRY FREE

NUT FREE

PALEO DIET

Guacamole

The smooth, creamy texture and bright green flesh of avocados make this guacamole a hit, while the healthy fat nourishes your body. Serve with sliced vegetables for an even healthier option.

Prep Time
15 minutes

Makes
8–12 servings

INGREDIENTS

3 avocados
$^1/_2$ large tomato, diced
$^1/_2$ red onion, chopped
2 garlic cloves, crushed
juice of 1 small lime
$^1/_2$ tsp sea salt, or to taste
$^1/_4$ tsp black pepper
$^1/_4$ tsp turmeric

METHOD

1 Split the avocados, and remove the stones. Scoop the flesh into a medium bowl, and mash with a fork until smooth with some small chunks.

2 Add the tomato, red onion, garlic, lime juice, sea salt, black pepper, and turmeric, and mix until combined.

3 Serve immediately, or keep in an airtight container in the fridge for up to 6 hours.

Variations

Sun-Dried Tomato Guacamole

FULL DIET

Omit the lime juice and turmeric, and replace the tomato with 15 sun-dried tomatoes, rehydrated and chopped. Replace the red onion with 75g (2$^1/_2$oz) palm hearts, diced. Add 2 tablespoons of grated Pecorino or Parmesan cheese and 1 tablespoon of capers. Continue as directed.

Pesto Guacamole

STAGE 4

Omit the lime juice and turmeric, and replace the tomato with 30 basil leaves, cut into ribbons. Replace the red onion with 2 tablespoons of pine nuts, soaked in water overnight. Continue as directed.

Basil

Easy Chicken Stir-Fry

This stir-fry is simple, quick, and satisfying. It's a great way to use up leftover chicken and vegetables too.

Prep Time
10 minutes

Cook Time
20 minutes

Makes
4 servings

INGREDIENTS

2 tbsp coconut oil or animal fat
1 onion, chopped
1 garlic clove, crushed
450g (1lb) chicken meat, preferably dark, sliced into strips
1 tsp sea salt
1 tsp ground black pepper
150g (5$\frac{1}{2}$oz) broccoli florets
1 carrot, grated
juice of 1 small lime
4 tbsp shredded, unsweetened coconut
Coconut aminos (soy sauce substitute)

METHOD

1 In a medium frying pan, melt the coconut oil over a medium-high heat. Add the onion, and sauté for 5 minutes, or until translucent.

2 Add the garlic, and sauté for 3 minutes, or until fragrant.

3 Season the chicken with $\frac{1}{2}$ teaspoon of sea salt and $\frac{1}{2}$ teaspoon of black pepper. Add the chicken to the pan, and cook for 7–10 minutes, or until no longer pink in the centre.

4 Add the broccoli, carrot, and lime juice, sprinkle with the remaining sea salt and black pepper, and cook for 5 minutes.

5 To serve, sprinkle 1 tablespoon of coconut over each serving and top with coconut aminos to taste.

Prawns

Variation

Spicy Prawn Stir-Fry

STAGE 5

Use 450g (1lb) large prawns instead of the chicken. For the vegetables, sauté the onions and garlic as directed, and use 70g (2$\frac{1}{2}$oz) pak choi, 70g (2$\frac{1}{2}$oz) cabbage, and 70g (2$\frac{1}{2}$oz) mangetout instead of the broccoli and carrots. Use lime juice and add $\frac{1}{4}$ teaspoon of ground coriander, $\frac{1}{4}$ teaspoon of ground ginger, and 1 pinch of crushed dried chillies (optional). Sprinkle with chopped cashews instead of flaked coconut and coconut aminos.

DAIRY FREE

PALEO DIET

Tex-Mex Pulled Pork Burritos

In this dish, tender, slow-cooked pork is blanketed in a soft wrap and smothered with a mildly spiced Tex-Mex style sauce.

Prep Time
15 minutes

Cook Time
15 minutes

Makes
8 servings

INGREDIENTS

2 tbsp sea salt

1 tsp black pepper

2 tsp paprika

$1/2$ tsp mustard powder

$1^1/2$ tsp ground cumin

$1/2$ tsp chipotle powder

4kg (8lb) bone-in Boston butt pork shoulder

2 tbsp ghee or animal fat

750ml (1$^1/4$ pints) home-made chicken stock

1 large onion, chopped

3 garlic cloves, chopped

2 tsp chilli powder

750g (1lb 10oz) passata

240ml (8fl oz) cider vinegar

1 tsp ground cumin

120ml (4fl oz) raw honey

15g ($^1/2$oz) coriander leaves

8 Almond Flour Wraps

METHOD

1 Preheat the oven to 160°C (325°F/Gas 3). In a small bowl, combine the sea salt, black pepper, paprika, mustard powder, cumin, and chipotle powder. Rub the spice mixture into the pork shoulder.

2 Place a large stockpot over a medium-high heat, and add the ghee. Add the pork shoulder, and cook, turning occasionally, for 6 minutes, or until lightly browned on all sides.

3 Place the pork fat-side up and add 500ml (16fl oz) chicken stock, the onion and garlic. Cover, and cook for 4 hours, or until the meat shreds easily with a fork. Remove from the oven, allow to cool completely, and pull the meat from the bone.

4 Place the pan over a medium-high heat, bring to the boil, and reduce the heat to medium-low. Add the chilli powder, passata, cider vinegar, remaining chicken stock, cumin, honey, and coriander, and cook uncovered for 20 minutes, or until the sauce has reduced. Working in small batches, process the sauce in a blender until smooth.

5 To serve, place $^1/8$ of the pork in the centre of 1 Almond Flour Wrap, fold in the edges, and roll up the wrap, away from you. Smother the burritos with sauce.

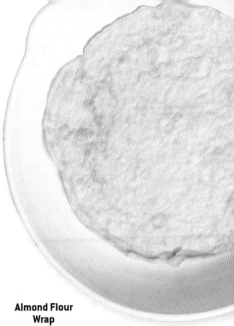

**Almond Flour
Wrap**

Component

Almond Flour
Wraps

STAGE 4

INGREDIENTS
5 large free-range eggs
3 tbsp water
¼ tsp sea salt
60g (2oz) almond flour

METHOD
1 In a medium bowl, whisk together the eggs, water, and sea salt. Slowly whisk in the almond flour until the batter is well combined and smooth. Cover and leave in the fridge for 10 minutes to allow the batter to thicken.

2 Heat a large frying pan over a medium heat, brush with ghee, add 1 tablespoon of batter, and swirl the skillet to coat with the batter.

3 Cook for 1 minute, or until the wrap is set and firm to the touch. Using a spatula, carefully flip the wrap, and cook for another 30 seconds. Transfer to a plate, and repeat with the remaining batter.

DAIRY FREE **NUT FREE** **PALEO DIET**

Apple Pie Stewed Apples

Nothing beats the warm, spiced flavour of apple pie. And these thin, melting slices of fruit taste just as great, without the crust. Even better, serve them with pork or butternut squash pancakes.

Prep Time
10 minutes

Cook Time
30 minutes

Makes
6 servings

INGREDIENTS

- 1.5kg (about 3lb) red eating apples, such as Macintosh or Gala, cored, peeled, and cut into 5mm (1/4in) slices
- 2 tbsp water
- 2 tbsp ghee or animal fat
- 1/2 tsp ground cinnamon
- 1 tsp ground allspice
- 1/2 tsp ground nutmeg
- 1/2 tsp ground ginger
- 1/4 tsp ground cloves
- 1/8 tsp ground cardamom
- 1/8 tsp sea salt

METHOD

1 In a large saucepan, combine the apples, water, ghee, cinnamon, allspice, nutmeg, ginger, cloves, cardamom, and sea salt. Cover, place over a medium heat, and cook for 30 minutes, stirring every 5 minutes.

2 Uncover, and cook for another 5 minutes to reduce any liquid. Remove from the heat and allow the apples to cool for 5 minutes before serving.

3 If not using immediately, allow to cool completely before storing tightly covered in the fridge for up to 1 week.

Variation

Chamomile Ginger Apple Sauce

STAGE 5

INGREDIENTS

- 1 chamomile teabag
- 240ml (8fl oz) hot water
- 8 green apples, peeled, cored, and quartered
- 1 tsp lemon zest
- 60ml (2fl oz) lemon juice
- 1/2 tsp sea salt
- 1 tbsp fresh root ginger, peeled and finely grated
- 60ml (2fl oz) raw honey

METHOD

1 Steep 1 chamomile teabag in hot water for 10 minutes, and discard the teabag.

2 In a medium stockpot over a high heat, combine the apples, lemon zest, lemon juice, sea salt, brewed tea, and ginger. Bring to the boil, reduce the heat to medium-low, and simmer for 25 minutes, or until the apples are tender.

3 Remove from the heat, and mash the apples with a potato masher, or process in small batches in a food processor or blender until smooth. When the desired texture is achieved, stir in the honey.

Apple Pie Stewed Apples

**DAIRY
FREE**

Baked Cinnamon Walnut Apples

Tender baked apples are topped with crunchy nuts and cinnamon. This recipe is a great way to use up a glut of apples in season.

**Golden
Delicious
apples**

Prep Time
50 minutes

Cook Time
35 minutes

Makes
4 servings

INGREDIENTS

4 large apples, such as
  Golden Delicious

4 tsp ghee or animal fat

4 tsp raw honey

2 tsp ground cinnamon

30g (1oz) chopped
  walnuts

120ml (4fl oz) boiling
  water

METHOD

1 Preheat the oven to 190°C (375°F/ Gas 5).

2 Using an apple corer or paring knife, core the apples, leaving 1.25cm (½in) of apple intact at the bottom. Carve out the centre hole to about 2.5cm (1in) in diameter.

3 In a small bowl, combine the ghee, honey, cinnamon, and walnuts. Evenly divide this mixture among the apples, spooning it into each central hole.

4 Place the apples in an 20 × 20cm (8 × 8in) baking dish, and pour the boiling water into the bottom. Bake on the middle oven shelf for 35 minutes, or until the apples are just tender.

5 Remove from the oven, baste the apples with the juices, and allow to cool for 5 minutes before serving.

Variation

Baked Apples with Cinnamon, Walnuts, Raisins, and Yogurt

Add 4 teaspoons of raisins to the filling, and top the apples with 2 tablespoons of home-made yogurt when ready to serve.

FULL
DIET

Anytime Smoothies

Smooth, creamy, and refreshing, this balanced smoothie is tasty any time of day. You can vary the berry types and use more of your favourites, or whatever is in season.

Prep Time
5 minutes

Makes
2 servings

INGREDIENTS

240ml (8fl oz) home-made yogurt

60ml (2fl oz) home-made almond milk

60g (2oz) fresh or frozen raspberries, blackberries, blueberries, or strawberries

1 banana, sliced

30g (1oz) ripe avocado

1/4 tsp pure vanilla extract

METHOD

1 In a blender, blend the yogurt, almond milk, berries, banana, avocado, and vanilla extract for 20 seconds, or until the desired consistency is reached.

2 Serve immediately, or store tightly covered in the fridge for up to 2 days.

Variations

Cherry Almond Chiller

STAGE 6

Blend 150g (5½oz) fresh or frozen cherries, 240ml (8fl oz) home-made almond milk, 3 tablespoons of raw soaked and dried whole almonds, 1 tablespoon of raw honey, ½ teaspoon of pure almond extract, and 1 tablespoon of coconut oil.

PB&J Smoothie

STAGE 6

Blend 175g (6oz) fresh or frozen trimmed and sliced strawberries, 240ml (8fl oz) home-made almond milk, 2 tablespoons of organic natural peanut butter, 1 tablespoon of raw honey, and 1 sliced banana.

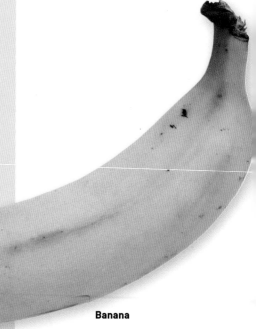

Banana

Roasted Brussels Sprout Apple Salad

Caramelized Brussels sprouts, lemony vinaigrette, crunchy almonds, and naturally sweet red apples – this salad is a clean, fresh start to any meal. It's also excellent as a meal in itself.

Prep Time
15 minutes

Cook Time
15 minutes

Makes
2 servings

INGREDIENTS

- 250g (9oz) Brussels sprouts, stems removed, quartered
- $^3/_4$ tsp sea salt
- 2 tbsp ghee or animal fat
- 60g (2oz) home-made butter, sliced
- 2 tbsp fresh lemon juice
- $^1/_8$ tsp black pepper
- 1 red apple, cored, quartered, and cut into 5mm ($^1/_4$in) slices
- 1 thin slice of red onion
- 150g (5oz) baby spinach
- 3 tbsp slivered almonds
- 3 tbsp shaved Pecorino cheese

METHOD

1 Preheat the oven to 180°C (350°F/Gas 4).

2 In a small bowl, toss together the Brussels sprouts, $^1/_4$ teaspoon of sea salt, and the ghee. Transfer to a large cast-iron ovenproof frying pan or roasting tin, and roast on the top shelf of the oven for 15 minutes, or until browned.

3 While the sprouts are roasting, place a heavy-based saucepan over a medium heat and melt the butter, whisking regularly, for 5 minutes. Remove from the heat and strain into a small bowl. Add the lemon juice, $^1/_4$ teaspoon of sea salt, and the black pepper, and stir to combine.

4 Remove the Brussels sprouts from the oven, and cool for 5 minutes.

5 In a medium bowl, combine the roasted Brussels sprouts, red apple, red onion, baby spinach, almonds, remaining sea salt, and Pecorino cheese.

6 Drizzle the dressing over, and toss to coat well. Divide the salad between two plates, and serve.

Brussels sprouts

NUT FREE

Scallops Piccata

Sweet caramelized scallops balance nicely with salty caperberries and a rich, tangy lemon butter sauce. Fresh tomatoes and flat-leaf parsley lend colour to the finished dish.

Prep Time
10 minutes

Cook Time
10 minutes

Makes
4 servings

INGREDIENTS

16 dry king scallops

$^1/_4$ tsp sea salt

$^1/_4$ tsp black pepper

2 tbsp ghee

2 garlic cloves

$^1/_2$ small onion, chopped

120ml (4fl oz) home-made chicken stock

10g ($^1/_4$oz) chopped flat-leaf parsley

60ml (2fl oz) fresh lemon juice

2 tbsp caperberries

180g (6oz) diced tomato

2 tbsp home-made butter

METHOD

1 Pull the side muscles off the scallops, rinse under cold water, and pat dry. Season both sides of the scallops evenly with sea salt and black pepper.

2 Heat a large frying pan over a medium-high heat, add the ghee, and swirl the pan to coat. Add the scallops, and cook for 3 minutes each side, or until brown and caramelized. Transfer the scallops to a plate.

3 Reduce the heat to medium, add the garlic and onion, and cook for 2 minutes, or until the onions are just softened.

4 Add the chicken stock and cook for 2 minutes, or until reduced by half.

5 Add the flat-leaf parsley, lemon juice, caperberries, tomato, and butter, and swirl the pan until the butter is incorporated into the sauce.

6 Return the scallops to the pan, turn to coat, and serve covered with the sauce.

Scallops

Q&A

What's the difference between wet and dry scallops?

Fishmongers typically sell dry and wet scallops. If they're not labelled as such, be sure to ask. Dry scallops are fresher, have superior flavour, and sear better when cooked. Wet scallops have usually been treated with sodium tripolyphosphate (STP) to help retain moisture and extend their shelf life. This can make wet scallops difficult to brown when searing, mask their naturally sweet flavour, contribute to a rubbery texture, and release extra fluid during cooking. What's more, STP is a known contributor to inflammation and may impact your gut healing negatively. For best results, buy dry.

DAIRY FREE **NUT FREE**

Olive Raisin Tapenade

Naturally sweet raisins, fruity olives, salty capers, and tangy lemon combine in this amazing spread. Try it on some Three-Seed Crackers for a quick afternoon snack.

Prep Time
5 minutes

Makes
4 servings

INGREDIENTS

150g (5¹/₂oz) pitted black olives (no added ingredients)

2 tbsp caperberries, drained

30g (1oz) raisins (no sulphur)

1 tbsp extra virgin olive oil

¹/₂ garlic clove

1 tbsp basil leaves

1 tbsp lemon juice

¹/₄ tsp ground black pepper

METHOD

1 In a food processor fitted with a metal chopping blade, process the olives, caperberries, raisins, olive oil, garlic, basil, lemon juice, and black pepper until well blended.

2 Serve immediately, or store tightly covered in the fridge for up to 1 week.

Caperberries

Q&A

How else can I use Olive Raisin Tapenade?

Fold this tapenade into your Easy Avocado Omelette at breakfast. Spoon some on salmon or tuna cakes, add a dollop to Greek Lemon Vegetable Soup, add a topping to Lamb Burger Sliders, or spread on Oven-Roasted Moroccan Chicken or Lemon Rosemary Salmon. You also can use it as a dip with raw vegetables, Three-Seed Crackers, and Parmesan Rosemary Tuiles.

NUT FREE **PALEO DIET**

Chicken Thigh Puttanesca

Tender chicken, zesty tomato sauce, herbs, and tangy Parmesan make this fabulous one-pot meal a favourite.

Prep Time
15 minutes

Cook Time
15 minutes

Makes
4 servings

INGREDIENTS

4 tbsp ghee or animal fat

8 bone-in, skin-on chicken thighs, about 1.5kg (3lb) in total

1¹/₂ tsp sea salt

4 garlic cloves, chopped

1 large onion, chopped

60g (2oz) caperberries

350g (12oz) tomatoes, chopped

4 oil-packed anchovy fillets, minced or crushed in a pestle and mortar

1 litre (1³/₄ pints) home-made chicken stock

25g (1oz) basil leaves, chopped

2 tbsp oregano leaves, chopped

15g (¹/₂oz) flat-leaf parsley, chopped

¹/₄ tsp ground black pepper

1kg (2¹/₄lb) passata

25g (1oz) grated Parmesan cheese (optional)

METHOD

1 Place a flameproof casserole over a medium heat. Add 2 tablespoons of ghee, and swirl to coat the bottom.

2 Pat the chicken thighs dry, and season with sea salt on both sides. Add the chicken, skin-side down, and cook for 3 minutes, or until lightly browned. Turn and cook for another 2 minutes, or until browned. Transfer the chicken to a plate.

3 Add the remaining ghee, the garlic, and onion to the pan, and cook, stirring frequently, for 5 minutes.

4 Add the caperberries, tomatoes, anchovies, chicken stock, basil, oregano, parsley, black pepper, and passata, and stir to combine.

5 Return the chicken to the pan, and cover with the sauce. Bring the sauce to the boil, cover, reduce the heat to medium-low, and simmer for 30 minutes, until it reaches 70°C (160°F). Top with the sauce and cheese.

Component

Home-made Passata

STAGE 1

Making your own home-made passata is simple. Here's how:

1 In a large stockpot over a medium-high heat, cook 2.7–4kg (6–8lb) cored and roughly chopped plum tomatoes for 10 minutes, or until softened.

2 Set a food mill fitted with the largest plate attachment that allows tomatoes but not seeds to pass through over a large bowl, and run the tomatoes through.

3 Completely cool the passata in an ice bath in the sink before storing tightly covered in non-reactive containers for up to 7 days in the fridge or for up to 1 year in the freezer.

Tomatoes

DAIRY FREE **PALEO DIET**

Dairy-Free Key Lime Mousse

So light, smooth, and tangy, if you close your eyes you can practically hear the waves crashing onto the tropical beach. This dessert gets its texture from avocados and bananas rather than dairy ingredients.

Prep Time
20 minutes + 1 hour chill time

Makes
4 servings

INGREDIENTS

60g (2oz) walnuts, soaked and dried

30g (1oz) unsweetened flaked coconut

2 ripe avocados, peeled

1 ripe banana, peeled

1 tsp lemon zest

2 tbsp fresh lemon juice

1 tbsp lime zest

60ml (2fl oz) fresh lime juice

1 tsp pure vanilla extract

60ml (2fl oz) raw honey

$1/4$ tsp sea salt

METHOD

1 In a food processor fitted with a metal chopping blade, or in a blender, pulse the walnuts and coconut until they reach a crumb texture. (Or chop by hand using a knife.) Transfer the mixture to a bowl, and set aside.

2 In the food processor or blender, process the avocados, banana, lemon zest, lemon juice, lime zest, lime juice, vanilla extract, honey, and sea salt until smooth. (Or combine by hand with a fork or potato masher.) Chill in the fridge for at least 1 hour.

3 To serve, place $1/4$ of the crust mixture in the bottom of each of 4 cups or mugs, and top with $1/4$ of the mousse. Store unused cups tightly covered in the fridge for up to 1 week, or freeze for up to 1 month.

Variation

STAGE 6

Dairy-Free Raspberry Avocado Mousse

Place 2 peeled ripe avocados, 1 frozen peeled banana, 175g (6oz) frozen raspberries, 1 tablespoon of home-made coconut milk or home-made nut milk, 60ml (2fl oz) raw honey, and 1 teaspoon of fresh lemon juice in a food processer fitted with a metal blade, and process until smooth. Fill cups or mugs as directed with the coconut walnut crumbs, and top with raspberry avocado mousse.

DAIRY FREE **PALEO DIET**

Seasonal Mixed-Berry Crostata

This open baked crostata features a crispy, free-form crust. Sweet, tangy, seasonal fruit with a hint of cinnamon provides the filling.

Prep Time
15 minutes

Cook Time
50 minutes

Makes
8 servings

INGREDIENTS

350g (12oz) fresh seasonal blueberries, raspberries, blackberries, and/or chopped strawberries

1 tsp ground cinnamon

2 tbsp raw honey

1 tsp coconut flour

350g (12oz) almond flour

$1/4$ tsp baking soda

$1/4$ tsp sea salt

60g (2oz) coconut oil, cold, cut into small pieces

1 large egg

METHOD

1 Preheat the oven to 160°C (325°F/Gas 3).

2 In a small bowl, toss the berries with $1/2$ teaspoon of cinnamon, 1 tablespoon of raw honey, and the coconut flour. Set aside.

3 In a medium bowl, combine the almond flour, the remaining cinnamon, baking soda, and sea salt. Add the coconut oil, remaining honey, and egg, and stir to form a moist dough ball.

4 Place the dough in the centre of a 23cm (9in) pie dish, and press the dough to spread evenly across the bottom and up the sides. Add the berry mixture to the middle of the dough, and carefully fold the sides of dough down over the berry mixture to cover the edges. (It's okay if the dough breaks in places while folding.)

5 Bake on the middle oven shelf for about 50 minutes, or until the crust is uniformly brown and crisp.

Variation

Cherry Crostata

STAGE 6

Substitute 350g (12oz) fresh, stemmed, pitted, and halved cherries for the fresh berries. Continue as directed.

Cherries

DAIRY FREE

NUT FREE

Honey Bombs

These little dessert balls of honey and coconut are rich in healthy saturated fats. They're fun and easy to make, even for kids.

Prep Time
10 minutes

Makes
16 pieces

INGREDIENTS

350g (12oz) coconut butter or cream

20g (³/₄oz) unsweetened flaked coconut

30g (1oz) coconut flour

60ml (2fl oz) raw honey

METHOD

1 In a medium bowl, using a firm spatula, combine the coconut cream, flaked coconut, coconut flour, and honey.

2 Form the mixture into "bombs", by rolling a tablespoon of the mixture into balls with your hands.

3 Store tightly covered in the fridge for up to 3 months, or freeze for up 6 months.

Variation

Chocolate Honey Bombs

STAGE 6

Combine 20g (³/₄oz) cocoa powder and 1 teaspoon of honey, form into balls, and proceed as described. Make sure you've had 6 months with no digestive symptoms before attempting to reintroduce cocoa, because it can cause digestive distress.

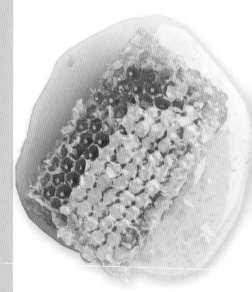

Honey

" To make your own coconut flour, pulse 20g (³/₄oz) unsweetened flaked coconut in a food processor fitted with a metal chopping blade until it reaches the consistency of flour. "

DAIRY FREE

NUT FREE

PALEO DIET

Gingered Vanilla Honey Drops

These gut-friendly sweets are a satisfying balance of sweet, sour, and spicy. The raw honey delivers antimicrobial benefits, the anti-inflammatory ginger relaxes and soothes the GI tract, and both deliver powerful antioxidants.

Prep Time
5 minutes

Cook Time
15 minutes

Makes
50 drops

INGREDIENTS

240ml (8fl oz) raw honey
60ml (2fl oz) cider vinegar
$^{1}/_{2}$ tsp ground ginger
$^{1}/_{4}$ tsp pure vanilla extract

METHOD

1 In a small saucepan over a medium-high heat, whisk together the honey, cider vinegar, and ginger. Bring to the boil, and cook until the liquid reaches 140C° (275°F) on a sugar thermometer.

2 Remove from the heat, and set aside for 1 minute. Gently stir in the vanilla extract.

3 Pour the mixture onto a baking sheet lined with baking parchment, or into candy moulds, and chill in the fridge for 20 minutes.

4 Cut or break the sweets into small pieces (if not using moulds). Store in a tightly covered container in layers separated by baking parchment.

" As long as it's unpasteurized, raw honey has an unlimited shelf life. Raw honey has a low water content and high acidity, which makes a very unfavourable environment for bacteria growth. To maintain the quality of raw honey, keep it dry and tightly sealed at room temperature, such as in a kitchen cupboard. "

FULL
DIET

STAGE 5

STAGE 6

FULL
DIET

DAIRY FREE   **NUT FREE**

Honey Sage Sausage Patties

Semi-sweet and savoury, these "breakfast burgers" feature a hint of honey and fragrant, warm sage – pure deliciousness.

Prep Time
5 minutes

Cook Time
10 minutes

Makes
8 servings

INGREDIENTS

450g (1lb) minced pork
2 tsp raw honey
1 tsp mustard powder
1 tsp dried rubbed sage
1 tsp onion powder
$1/4$ tsp garlic powder
$1/2$ tsp ground black pepper
$1/2$ tsp sea salt
3 tbsp ghee or animal fat

METHOD

1 In a medium bowl, combine the pork, honey, mustard powder, sage, onion powder, garlic powder, black pepper, and sea salt.

2 Form into eight 1.25cm ($1/2$in) patties.

3 In a large frying pan over a medium heat, heat the ghee, swirling to coat the bottom of the pan.

4 Add the sausage patties, cover, and cook for 5 minutes.

5 Uncover, carefully turn over the patties, re-cover, and cook for another 5 minutes, or until the juices run clear.

Variation

Spicy Italian Chicken Sausage Patties

FULL DIET

Substitute minced chicken for the pork; add 1 teaspoon of dried basil, $1/2$ teaspoon of paprika, $1/2$ teaspoon of crushed dried chillies, $1/4$ teaspoon of ground fennel seeds, and $1/4$ teaspoon of dried oregano, and reduce the black pepper to $1/4$ teaspoon.

Dried red chillies

NUT
FREE

Sausage, Egg, and Cheese Sandwich

You won't miss fast food when you can make this easy, speedy sandwich that's gooey, warm, satisfying – and gut friendly.

Prep Time
5 minutes

Cook Time
3 minutes

Makes
1 serving

INGREDIENTS

1 large free-range egg

$1/8$ tsp sea salt

1 tsp ghee or animal fat

1 slice mature Cheddar cheese

2 slices of grain-free bread, toasted, or 1 Cheddar Chive Biscuit, halved

1 Honey Sage Sausage Patty, cooked

METHOD

1 In a small bowl, whisk the egg and sea salt until frothy.

2 In a small frying pan, heat the ghee over a medium heat. Add the egg, and cook for 2–3 minutes, continually moving the cooked egg towards the middle of the pan with a spatula, until no liquid egg remains.

3 Place the Cheddar slice on one piece of bread, top with the Honey Sage Sausage Patty, add the egg, and then top with the remaining slice of bread.

Variation

Italian Sausage Egg Sandwich

FULL
DIET

INGREDIENTS

$1/2$ small onion, chopped

$1/2$ small green pepper, deseeded and diced

$1/2$ garlic clove, crushed

1 tbsp ghee

1 Spicy Italian Chicken Sausage Patty

1 large free-range egg

2 slices of Parmesan or Pecorino cheese

2 slices of grain-free bread, toasted

METHOD

1 In a small frying pan over a medium heat, cook the onion, green pepper, and garlic in ghee for 5 minutes, or until softened.

2 Reheat the cooked Spicy Italian Chicken Sausage Patty.

3 Cook the egg as directed in step 2.

4 Top the sausage patty with the Parmesan cheese, egg, peppers, onion, and garlic. Place between slices of toasted grain-free bread.

Cheddar Chive Biscuits

These light and flaky, grain-free Southern-style biscuits are related to cheese scones. Try them with Sausage Gravy or just home-made butter.

Prep Time
25 minutes

Cook Time
20 minutes

Makes
4 servings of
2 biscuits

INGREDIENTS

450g (1lb) almond flour
$^1/_2$ tsp sea salt
$^1/_2$ tsp baking soda
75g (2$^1/_2$oz) coconut oil, chilled
60g (2oz) grated Cheddar cheese
20g ($^3/_4$oz) snipped chives
2 large free-range eggs

METHOD

1 Preheat the oven to 200°C (400°F/Gas 6). In a medium bowl, combine the almond flour, sea salt, and baking soda.

2 In another medium bowl, whisk together the coconut oil, Cheddar, chives, and eggs.

3 Gradually add the dry ingredients to the wet ingredients, and stir until a dough forms.

4 Place the dough on one side of a piece of baking parchment. Fold the paper over on top of dough, and roll out the dough to 2cm ($^3/_4$in) thick. If the dough is sticky, dust with additional almond flour.

5 Using a 5cm (2in) cookie cutter, or a glass, cut out 8 biscuits. Place on a baking sheet lined with baking parchment, and bake on the middle shelf for 20 minutes, or until browned. Cool before serving.

Accompaniment
Sausage Gravy

INGREDIENTS

450g (1lb) minced pork
1 tbsp garlic powder
1 tbsp onion powder
2 tbsp chopped sage
1 tbsp chopped thyme
1 tsp ground black pepper
1 tsp sea salt
1 tbsp ghee
1 litre (1³/₄ pints) home-made
   chicken stock

FULL DIET

METHOD

1 In a medium bowl, combine the pork, garlic powder, onion powder, sage, thyme, ground black pepper, and sea salt.

2 Spread the pork mixture evenly on a baking sheet, and bake on the middle oven shelf for 15 minutes, or until cooked through.

3 Remove from the oven, transfer the pork and fat to a medium saucepan, and place over a medium-high heat.

4 Add the ghee and stock, and bring to the boil. Cover, reduce heat to medium-low, and simmer for 15 minutes.

5 Remove from the heat, and purée ¹/₃ of the gravy with a hand-held blender.

**Sausage
Gravy**

DAIRY FREE

PALEO DIET

Grainless Granola

Nuts and seeds are a staple of the healthy gut diet, and this recipe combines their crunchiness with other gut-supporting ingredients into a delicious, gluten-free, grain-free granola.

Prep Time
5 minutes

Cook Time
40 minutes

Makes
12 servings

INGREDIENTS

75g (2^1/$_2$oz) unsweetened shredded coconut

50g (1^3/$_4$oz) raw walnuts

75g (2^1/$_2$oz) raw almonds

75g (2^1/$_2$oz) raw hazelnuts

100g (3^1/$_2$oz) raw Brazil nuts

100g (3^1/$_2$oz) raw cashews

50g (1^3/$_4$oz) raw pecans

75g (2^1/$_2$oz) raw shelled sunflower seeds

75g (2^1/$_2$oz) raw shelled pumpkin seeds

75ml (2^1/$_2$fl oz) raw honey

60g (2oz) coconut oil

2 tsp pure vanilla extract

1 tsp ground cinnamon

^{1}/$_4$ tsp sea salt

85g (3oz) unsweetened dried apples, peaches, apricots, cherries, raisins, or currants (no sulphur)

75g (2^1/$_2$oz) raw sesame seeds

METHOD

1 Preheat the oven to 150°C (300°F/Gas 2). In a medium bowl, mix the coconut, nuts, pumpkin seeds, sunflower seeds, honey, coconut oil, vanilla extract, cinnamon, and sea salt.

2 Transfer to a large baking sheet, spread in an even layer, and bake on the middle oven shelf for 20 minutes.

3 Add the dried fruit and sesame seeds, stir to combine, and bake for another 20 minutes, or until everything is toasted.

4 Remove from the oven, and allow to cool completely.

5 Break the clusters into smaller pieces as needed, and store in an airtight container in a cool, dry place.

❝ All nuts must be properly soaked and dried, and roughly chopped. ❞

Q&A

How else can I use Grainless Granola?

This versatile granola is great as a breakfast cereal with home-made almond milk, sprinkled on top of home-made yogurt with ground cinnamon and fresh berries for a snack, or on its own by the handful. On the move? Pack some granola to go. It doesn't need to be kept in the fridge, so it won't deteriorate while you're out and about.

Mixed nuts

DAIRY FREE **NUT FREE** **PALEO DIET**

Grilled Vegetable Frittata

Grilling adds a smoky flavour to this savoury one-pot dish with its colourful mix of antioxidant-rich vegetables. It's easy to make in advance and can be enjoyed hot or cold.

Prep Time
20 minutes

Cook Time
45 minutes

Makes
8 servings

INGREDIENTS

- 2 garlic cloves, crushed
- ½ tsp sea salt
- 1 small courgette, cut into 2.5cm (1in) rounds
- 1 small yellow courgette, cut into 2.5cm (1in) rounds
- 1 orange pepper, ribs and seeds removed, cut into 2.5cm (1in) slices
- 1 red pepper, ribs and seeds removed, quartered
- 50g (1¾oz) spring onions, sliced
- 1 medium red onion, cut into 2.5cm (1in) slices
- 1 tbsp ghee or animal fat
- 12 large eggs
- 10g (¼oz) basil, chopped
- 10g (¼oz) flat-leaf parsley, chopped
- 50g (1¾oz) grated Parmesan cheese

METHOD

1 Preheat the grill on a medium setting. Preheat the oven to 180°C (350°F/Gas 4). Lightly grease a medium ovenproof frying pan with ghee.

2 In a medium bowl, combine the garlic, sea salt, and vegetables. Drizzle with ghee, and toss to coat.

3 Place the vegetables on the grill and cook for 3 minutes each side. Transfer to a plate, and then chop and add to the frying pan. Leave to cool for 15 minutes.

4 In a large bowl, whisk together the eggs, basil, parsley, and cheese. Pour the mixture over the vegetables in the frying pan, place over a medium-low heat, and cook without stirring for 5 minutes.

5 Transfer the pan to the oven, and bake for 40 minutes or until set. Brown under the grill for 2 minutes.

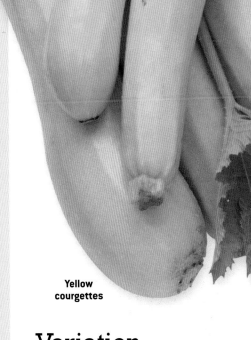

Yellow courgettes

Variation

Roasted Vegetable Frittata

FULL DIET

Preheat the oven to 230°C (450°F/Gas 8). Spread the coated vegetables evenly over a large baking sheet, and roast on the middle oven shelf for 10 minutes. Remove from the oven, and allow to cool before roughly chopping and combining with the egg mixture as directed.

DAIRY FREE   **NUT FREE**   **PALEO DIET**

Chopped Cobb Salad

A main-course salad made with crispy greens, hard-boiled eggs, tender chicken, refreshing tomatoes, and sharp red onion. This flexible combo salad gives you a little bit of everything.

Prep Time
15 minutes

Makes
2 servings

INGREDIENTS

60ml (2fl oz) extra virgin olive oil

60ml (2fl oz) lemon juice

1 tbsp chopped basil, coriander, or flat-leaf parsley

$1/4$ tsp sea salt

$1/4$ tsp black pepper

175g (6oz) romaine lettuce, finely chopped

125g ($4^1/2$oz) cooked chicken, diced or shredded (from stock chicken)

1 tomato, diced

$1/2$ small red onion, diced

1 avocado, peeled, and diced

2 hard-boiled eggs, peeled and sliced

METHOD

1 In a small bowl, whisk together the olive oil, lemon juice, herbs, sea salt, and black pepper. Set aside.

2 In a large bowl, combine the romaine lettuce, chicken, tomato, red onion, and avocado.

3 Add the dressing to the salad, and toss to coat.

4 Divide the dressed salad evenly between 2 bowls, place the hard-boiled eggs on the side, and serve.

" To hard-boil eggs, place the eggs in a large saucepan, cover with water, place over a high heat, and bring to the boil. Reduce the heat to medium-high, and simmer for 9 minutes. Drain and run cold water over the eggs until cool. "

Calming Kale Salad

Kale is a true nutritional powerhouse. Massaging the dressing into the kale "calms" and tenderizes the leaves in this lemony, nutty salad. They "relax" even more, the longer the salad sits.

Prep Time
15 minutes

Makes
2 servings

INGREDIENTS

$1/2$ garlic clove, crushed

240ml (8fl oz) fresh lemon juice

240ml (8fl oz) extra virgin olive oil

$1/4$ tsp sea salt

$1/4$ tsp ground black pepper

450g (1lb) kale, large tough stems discarded, chopped

125g ($4^1/2$oz) grilled or shredded chicken, chopped

1 carrot, grated

30g (1oz) chopped raw walnuts

30g (1oz) spring onions, green part only, thinly sliced

30g (1oz) dried currants (no sulphur)

2 thin slices of red onion

75g ($2^1/2$oz) Brie cheese, rind off, diced

METHOD

1 In a small bowl, whisk together the garlic, lemon juice, olive oil, sea salt, and black pepper.

2 Place the kale in a medium bowl, and drizzle the dressing over the top. Gently massage the dressing into the leaves for 5 minutes.

3 Add the chicken, carrots, walnuts, spring onions, currants, red onion, and Brie. Toss to combine, and serve.

4 Keep any unused dressing tightly covered in the fridge. Shake before serving.

Olive oil

NUT
FREE

Grilled Steak Salad

Crisp lettuce, rich and meaty grilled steak and portobellos, tomatoes, and a punchy dressing combine to create a salad that's perfect for a barbecue.

Prep Time
15 minutes

Cook Time
20 minutes

Makes
2 servings

INGREDIENTS

- 2 portobello mushrooms, stems removed
- 1 tbsp ghee or animal fat
- $1/2$ tsp sea salt
- $1/8$ tsp ground black pepper
- 350g (12oz) top sirloin steak, 2.5–3.75cm (1–1$1/2$in) thick
- 250g (9oz) romaine lettuce hearts, chopped
- 1 tomato, cored and sliced into 4
- $1/2$ avocado, peeled and sliced
- 2 thin slices red onion
- 120ml (4fl oz) Horsey Dressing

METHOD

1 Preheat the grill to a medium setting. Brush both sides of the portobello mushrooms with ghee, and sprinkle the mushrooms and steak with salt and pepper.

2 Grill for 7 minutes, rotating 90 degrees halfway through the cooking time. Turn over and cook for 7 minutes on the other side, again rotating 90 degrees halfway through.

3 Transfer the steak and mushrooms to separate plates, and let rest for 5 minutes before slicing thinly on the bias.

4 In a medium bowl, toss together the lettuce, tomato, avocado, red onion, steak, and mushrooms, and toss with Horsey Dressing to coat.

Dressing
Horsey Dressing

In a food processor fitted with a metal blade, process 400ml (14fl oz) home-made yogurt; 4 tablespoons of peeled, freshly grated horseradish root; 1 teaspoon of lemon juice; 30g (1oz) finely chopped spring onion, green parts only; $1/8$ teaspoon of black pepper; and $1/4$ teaspoon of sea salt until smooth. Keep tightly covered in the fridge until needed.

FULL
DIET

Portobello mushrooms

DAIRY FREE   NUT FREE   PALEO DIET

Seared Scallop Salad with Asian Vegetables

Tender, sweet scallops are the star in this salad. Crisp, garden-fresh vegetables and a refreshing, citrusy dressing complete this light but satisfying dish that's perfect for a summer dinner.

Prep Time
20 minutes

Cook Time
5 minutes

Makes
2 servings

INGREDIENTS

240ml (8fl oz) fresh orange juice

150ml (5fl oz) cider vinegar

100g (3^1/$_2$ oz) tahini paste

^{1}/$_2$ tsp salt (additive-free)

10g (^{1}/$_4$oz) fresh coriander leaves

1 garlic clove

240ml (8fl oz) extra virgin olive oil

1 small carrot, grated

1 small red pepper, ribs and seeds removed, thinly sliced

225g (8oz) Chinese leaves, thinly sliced

1 spring onion, thinly sliced on the bias

^{1}/$_2$ small red onion, thinly sliced

8 dry king scallops

^{1}/$_4$ tsp sea salt

1 tbsp ghee or animal fat

METHOD

1 In a blender, pulse the orange juice, cider vinegar, tahini paste, salt, coriander, and garlic to combine. Switch the blender to a low speed, and slowly drizzle in the olive oil.

2 In a medium bowl, combine the carrot, red pepper, Chinese leaves, spring onion, and red onion. Add the dressing, and toss to coat.

3 Remove the small side muscles from the scallops, rinse with cold water, and thoroughly pat dry. Sprinkle sea salt over the scallops.

4 Heat a medium frying pan over a medium-high heat, and add the ghee, swirling the pan to coat it. Gently add the scallops, and sear them for 1^1/$_2$ minutes, or until a golden crust forms on each side and the centre is translucent.

5 Divide the dressed salad between 2 plates, top each salad with 4 cooked scallops, and serve.

**NUT
FREE**

Wedge Salad with Ranch

Leafy lettuce, colourful, crunchy vegetables, and a creamy herb dressing makes for a quick and delicious salad. Throw in some grilled, poached, or shredded chicken, fish, or beef, or some hard-boiled eggs, for an added boost of protein.

Prep Time
15 minutes

Makes
4 servings

INGREDIENTS

- 1 head of romaine lettuce, soft leaves only
- 2 carrots, coarsely grated
- 150g (5$^1/_2$oz) cherry tomatoes, halved
- 120g (4oz) cucumber, peeled, seeded, halved lengthways and sliced
- 2 thin slices of red onion
- 240ml (8fl oz) home-made yogurt
- 1 tsp chopped dill
- 1 tsp chopped coriander
- 1 tsp chopped basil
- 1 tbsp chopped spring onion
- $^1/_2$ garlic clove, crushed
- 1 tsp cider vinegar
- $^1/_4$ tsp sea salt
- $^1/_4$ tsp ground black pepper
- 2 tbsp grated Pecorino cheese
- 120ml (4fl oz) extra virgin olive oil

METHOD

1 Remove the tough stems and core from the lettuce, and chop into quarters.

2 Place 1 lettuce wedge on each of 4 plates, and top each with the carrots, the cherry tomatoes, the cucumber, and $^1/_2$ slice of red onion.

3 In a small bowl, combine the yogurt, dill, coriander, basil, spring onion, garlic, vinegar, sea salt, ground black pepper, and cheese. Slowly whisk in the olive oil until combined. Or place all the ingredients in a glass jar with a lid and shake until well combined.

4 Drizzle each salad with dressing.

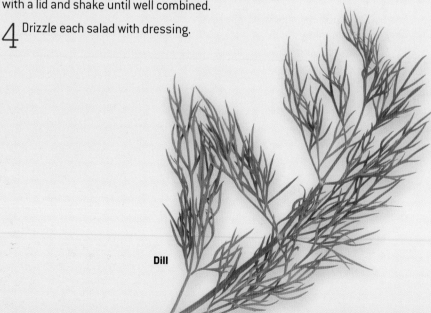

Dill

DAIRY FREE

Spring Tuna Niçoise Salad

This crispy, vibrant take on the traditional Mediterranean salad is pulled together by a tangy vinaigrette. You can substitute poached or canned salmon for the tuna, if preferred.

Prep Time
15 minutes

Makes
2 servings

INGREDIENTS

120ml (4fl oz) cider vinegar

120ml (4fl oz) cool water

60g (2oz) capers, chopped

75g (2^1/$_2$oz) Niçoise or Kalamata olives, pitted and chopped

3 tbsp mustard powder

1 tbsp flat-leaf parsley

^{1}/$_2$ tsp ground black pepper

120ml (4fl oz) extra virgin olive oil

350g (12oz) red and green lettuce leaves, chopped

1 small red pepper, deseeded, quartered, and thinly sliced

50g (1^3/$_4$oz) spring onions, thinly sliced

2 thin slices of red onion

60g (2oz) cucumber, peeled, seeded, halved, and sliced

85g (3oz) frozen artichoke hearts, thawed and quartered

75g (2^1/$_2$oz) cherry tomatoes, halved

75g (2^1/$_2$oz) French beans, cut into 2.5cm (1in) pieces

2 tsp slivered almonds, soaked and dried

160g (6oz) tuna packed in oil

METHOD

1 In a blender or a food processor fitted with a metal chopping blade, process the cider vinegar, water, capers, olives, mustard powder, flat-leaf parsley, and black pepper until smooth.

2 With the processor or blender set at a low speed, drizzle in the olive oil until combined.

3 In a medium bowl, combine the lettuce, red pepper, spring onions, red onion, cucumber, artichoke hearts, cherry tomatoes, French beans, almonds, and tuna.

4 Drizzle with 6 tablespoons of dressing, and toss to coat well. Divide the salad evenly between 2 plates.

Kalamata olives

DAIRY FREE **PALEO DIET**

Salmon Spinach Cobb Salad

This salad offers plenty of variety. Tender baby spinach, rich salmon, crunchy almonds, smooth avocado, and sweet grapes add up to a flavourful and satisfying no-cook meal.

Prep Time
15 minutes

Makes
2 servings

INGREDIENTS

150g (5^1/$_2$oz) baby spinach

170g (6oz) canned wild salmon, packed in its juice or oil

30g (1oz) almonds, soaked, dried, and chopped

^{1}/$_2$ avocado, peeled and sliced

75g (2^1/$_2$oz) red seedless grapes, halved

^{1}/$_2$ red onion, thinly sliced

2 plum tomatoes, quartered

50g (1^3/$_4$oz) cucumber, halved and thinly sliced

2 large free-range hard-boiled eggs, peeled and sliced

120ml (4fl oz) of Honey Mustard Vinaigrette

METHOD

1 Divide the baby spinach between 2 medium bowls.

2 Evenly divide the salmon, almonds, avocado, grapes, red onion, tomatoes, cucumber, eggs, and Honey Mustard Vinaigrette between the bowls, and serve.

Honey Mustard Vinaigrette

Dressing

Honey Mustard Vinaigrette

For 500ml (16fl oz) vinaigrette, place 120ml (4fl oz) raw honey, 120ml (4fl oz) cider vinegar, 120ml (4fl oz) extra virgin olive oil, 25g (scant 1 oz) mustard powder, 1 tablespoon of dried turmeric, 1 tablespoon of garlic powder, 2 teaspoons of onion powder, 1 teaspoon of ground black pepper, and 1 teaspoon of sea salt in a glass jar. Seal the lid tightly, and shake to combine.

STAGE 6

DAIRY FREE

PALEO DIET

Chunky Chicken Salad

Nothing beats a simple and refreshing chicken salad. Pair with two slices of Everyday Grain-Free Bread for a satisfying sandwich.

Prep Time
10 minutes

Makes
8 servings

INGREDIENTS

1 large free-range egg

1 tbsp fresh lemon juice

$^1/_4$ tsp mustard powder

$^1/_4$ tsp sea salt

240ml (8fl oz) extra virgin olive oil

350g (12oz) poached, grilled, or shredded chicken, cooled and chopped

75g (2$^1/_2$oz) red seedless grapes, quartered

30g (1oz) walnuts, soaked and dried, chopped

25g (scant 1oz) chopped spring onions

30g (1oz) celery, finely diced

2 tbsp flat-leaf parsley leaves, chopped

1 tbsp fresh lemon juice

1 tsp sea salt

$^1/_4$ tsp black pepper

METHOD

1 *For Mayo-Nays:* In a blender or a food processor fitted with a metal blade, combine the egg, lemon juice, mustard powder, and sea salt until smooth. On a low speed, slowly drizzle in the olive oil until emulsified.

2 In a medium bowl, combine the chicken, red grapes, walnuts, spring onions, celery, flat-leaf parsley, Mayo-Nays, lemon juice, sea salt, and black pepper.

3 Serve on bread. Keep any leftovers tightly covered in the fridge for up to 1 week.

Thai Tuna Salad

Variation

Thai Tuna Salad

STAGE 6

INGREDIENTS

450g (1lb) tuna packed
    in water or its own juices

$^1/_2$ small red pepper, ribs and
    seeds removed, diced

25g (scant 1oz) spring onions,
    chopped

30g (1oz) cucumber, peeled,
    deseeded and chopped

$^1/_2$ carrot, coarsely grated

2 tbsp chopped coriander leaves

1 tbsp chopped basil leaves

1 tbsp fresh lemon juice

60ml (2fl oz) Mayo-Nays

1 tsp sesame oil

1 tsp sea salt

$^1/_4$ tsp black pepper

METHOD

In a medium bowl, mix the tuna, red
pepper, spring onions, cucumber,
carrots, coriander, basil, lemon juice,
Mayo-Nays, sesame oil, sea salt, and
black pepper. Serve on bread. Store
any leftovers in the fridge.

NUT FREE

Chicken Cheddar Sandwiches

Slightly smoky grilled chicken, sharp melted Cheddar, toasted bread, and creamy coleslaw make this sandwich a solid addition to your culinary repertoire.

Prep Time
10 minutes

Cook Time
12 minutes

Makes
2 servings

INGREDIENTS

$^1/_4$ tsp sea salt

2 organic boneless, skinless chicken breasts, each about 175g (6oz)

4 slices grain-free bread

2 slices mature Cheddar cheese

60g (2oz) Creamy Coleslaw

METHOD

1 Preheat the grill to a medium setting. Sprinkle sea salt evenly all over the chicken breasts.

2 Grill the chicken for 6 minutes, rotating 90 degrees halfway through the cooking time. Turn the chicken, and cook for another 6 minutes, rotating 90 degrees halfway through the cooking time, or until the internal temperature reaches 70°C (160°F) and the juices run clear.

3 Place the grain-free bread on the grill, and lightly toast for 3 minutes.

4 Transfer the toast to separate plates, and top each of 2 pieces with 1 slice of Cheddar, followed by 1 chicken breast, and 30g (1oz) of Creamy Coleslaw, followed by the remaining pieces of toast.

Component

Creamy Coleslaw

FULL DIET

INGREDIENTS

120ml (4fl oz) home-made mayonnaise or aioli

2 tsp cider vinegar

2 tsp raw honey

$^1/_4$ tsp sea salt

200g (7oz) green cabbage, cored and shredded

30g (1oz) red cabbage, cored and shredded

1 carrot, coarsely grated

METHOD

1 In a small bowl, whisk together the mayonnaise or aioli, vinegar, honey, and sea salt. In a medium bowl, combine the green cabbage, red cabbage, and carrots.

2 Pour the dressing over the vegetables, and toss well. Keep any unused coleslaw tightly covered in the fridge. Makes about 400g (14oz).

Cider vinegar

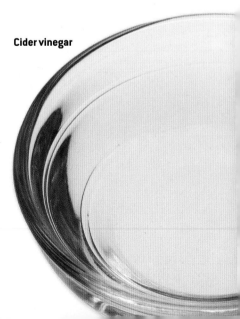

Turkey Reubens

The perfect balance of melted Swiss cheese, tangy sauerkraut, toasty bread, creamy dressing, and thinly sliced turkey, this fantastic deli sandwich hits the spot.

Prep Time
8 minutes

Cook Time
5 minutes

Makes
2 servings

INGREDIENTS

- 4 slices of grain-free bread
- 1 tbsp ghee
- 175g (6oz) cooked turkey or chicken, thinly sliced
- 100g (3½oz) home-made sauerkraut, drained
- 2 slices Emmental, or similar cheese
- 4 tbsp Russian Dressing

METHOD

1 Brush one side of each slice of grain-free bread with ghee to coat.

2 Heat a medium frying pan over a low heat. Place the bread slices, ghee-side down, in the pan. Divide the turkey between 2 slices of bread and top each with 50g (1¾oz) sauerkraut.

3 Place 1 cheese slice on each unused slice of bread.

4 Cover the frying pan, and cook for 3–5 minutes, or until the turkey and sauerkraut are warmed and the cheese has melted.

5 Uncover, and spread 2 tablespoons of Russian Dressing on each bread slice with the melted cheese.

6 Flip each bread slice with the cheese and dressing over onto a slice with turkey and sauerkraut. Transfer the sandwiches to a plate, and cut in half if desired.

Peeled and grated horseradish

Dressing

Russian Dressing

FULL DIET

INGREDIENTS

- 1 tbsp onion, finely chopped
- 240ml (8fl oz) home-made Mayo-Nays or aioli
- 60g (2oz) passata
- 1 tbsp raw honey
- 1 tbsp horseradish root, peeled and finely grated
- 1 tsp cider vinegar
- ¼ tsp sweet paprika
- ¼ tsp sea salt

METHOD

Whisk all the ingredients together in a small bowl. Makes about 240ml (8fl oz).

**DAIRY
FREE**

Lamb Burger Sliders

Satisfy your appetite with these juicy mini burgers, topped with creamy aioli for additional, luscious good-for-your-gut benefits.

Prep Time
20 minutes

Cook Time
10 minutes

Makes
4 servings of
2 burgers

INGREDIENTS

450g (1lb) minced lamb

1 tsp sea salt

16 slices gluten-free bread, lightly toasted

16 thin slices cucumber

8 thin slices tomato

4 thin slices red onion

Cumin Mint Aioli

METHOD

1 Form the lamb into 8 patties, and season both sides with sea salt.

2 Heat a large frying pan over a medium-high heat, add the patties, and cook for 3 minutes each side, or until the patties are cooked through and no pink remains.

3 Place 1 patty on 1 piece of bread. Top with 2 slices of cucumber, 1 slice of tomato, $1/2$ a slice of red onion, and 2 tablespoons of Cumin Mint Aioli. Add a second piece of bread, and serve.

Sauce

Cumin
Mint Aioli

FULL
DIET

INGREDIENTS
1 large free-range egg
1 tbsp fresh lemon juice
$^1/_4$ tsp mustard powder
$^1/_4$ tsp sea salt
$^1/_4$ tsp ground black pepper
10g ($^1/_4$oz) mint leaves
1 tsp ground cumin
240ml (8fl oz) extra virgin
   olive oil

METHOD
1 In a blender or a food processor
fitted with a metal blade, process the
egg, lemon juice, mustard powder, sea
salt, ground black pepper, mint leaves,
and cumin until smooth.

2 With the blender on a low speed,
slowly drizzle in the olive oil until
emulsified. Keep in the fridge, tightly
covered, for up to 1 week.

**Cumin Mint
Aioli**

NUT FREE

Margherita Pizza

You can't always eat pizza or even cheese on the healthy gut diet. But this GAPS-friendly, gluten-free version delivers a gooey, cheesy treat.

Prep Time
10 minutes

Cook Time
25 minutes

Makes
1 pizza serving 6

INGREDIENTS

115g (4oz) home-made coconut flour
115g (4oz) coconut oil
6 large free-range eggs
1 tsp sea salt
1 tsp garlic powder
1 tsp onion powder
125g (4$\frac{1}{2}$oz) passata
1 ripe tomato, sliced
85g (3oz) grated Monterey Jack cheese
1 tbsp grated Pecorino cheese
10g ($\frac{1}{4}$oz) basil leaves, chopped

METHOD

1 Preheat the oven to 180°C (350°F/ Gas 4). Line a baking sheet with baking parchment.

2 In a medium bowl, with a mixer on medium speed, combine the coconut flour, coconut oil, eggs, $\frac{3}{4}$ teaspoon of sea salt, the garlic powder, and onion powder for 4 minutes, or until soft and smooth.

3 Transfer the dough to the baking sheet, and press into a circle 23cm (9in) in diameter and 1.25cm ($\frac{1}{2}$in) thick. Bake for 10 minutes.

4 Remove the baking sheet from the oven, place a second piece of baking parchment on top of the pizza base, and carefully flip it over so that the new paper is now on the bottom. Bake for another 8 minutes.

5 Spread the passata evenly over the cooked crust. Top with the tomatoes, remaining salt, and cheese.

6 Bake for another 5 minutes, then serve, sprinkled with the basil.

Variations

Philly Cheesesteak Pizza

FULL DIET

Top the base evenly with 125g (4$\frac{1}{2}$oz) passata, 75g (2$\frac{1}{2}$oz) cooked and shredded beef, $\frac{1}{4}$ sautéed sliced onion, 30g (1oz) sliced chestnut button mushrooms, and $\frac{1}{2}$ small deseeded and sliced green pepper. Top with 60g (2oz) grated Cheddar cheese, and bake as directed.

Chicken Parmesan Pizza

FULL DIET

Top the base evenly with 125g (4$\frac{1}{2}$oz) passata, 60g (2oz) cooked and chopped chicken, and 45g (1$\frac{1}{2}$ oz) of shaved Parmesan cheese, and bake as directed. Top with 2 tablespoons of chopped basil leaves.

Cheddar cheese

DAIRY FREE

Tuna Cakes with Rémoulade

Golden, lemony, and moist, these tuna cakes will tame even the pickiest of fish eaters. Double the tuna cake size and you can use the cakes in a sandwich.

Prep Time
20 minutes

Cook Time
15 minutes

Makes
4 servings of 3 cakes

INGREDIENTS

180ml (6fl oz) home-made aioli or Mayo-Nays
1 tbsp wholegrain mustard
1 tbsp capers, drained
1 tbsp chopped red onion
1 tbsp spring onion, green part only, chopped
1 tsp cider vinegar
$^3/_4$ tsp sea salt
$^1/_4$ tsp ground black pepper
480g (18oz) canned tuna
3 large free-range eggs
1 small onion, finely diced
2 tbsp fresh lemon juice
3 tbsp flat-leaf parsley leaves, chopped
1 tsp crushed garlic
120ml (4fl oz) ghee or coconut oil

METHOD

1 *For Wholegrain Mustard Rémoulade:* In a food processor, process the aioli, mustard, capers, red onion, spring onion, cider vinegar, $^1/_4$ teaspoon of sea salt, and black pepper until just smooth.

2 In a medium bowl, combine the tuna, eggs, onion, lemon juice, flat-leaf parsley, garlic, and remaining $^1/_2$ teaspoon of sea salt. Form into 12 patties 2cm ($^3/_4$ in) thick.

3 In a large frying pan over a medium heat, heat 60ml (2fl oz) of ghee. Add 6 tuna cakes to the skillet, and cook for 3 minutes on each side, or until just browned. Transfer to a plate.

4 Heat the remaining ghee in the pan, and cook the remaining 6 tuna cakes.

5 Serve the cooked cakes with Wholegrain Mustard Rémoulade.

Side Dish

Warm Portobello, Red Pepper, and Basil Salad

STAGE 3

INGREDIENTS

60ml (2fl oz) ghee
3 large portobello mushrooms, stems removed, halved and thinly sliced
1 garlic clove, crushed
$^1/_2$ tsp sea salt
$^1/_4$ tsp ground black pepper
1 large red pepper, ribs and seeds removed, halved and thinly sliced
20g ($^3/_4$oz) chopped basil leaves

METHOD

1 In a large frying pan over a medium-high heat, heat the ghee. Add the mushrooms, and cook, stirring frequently, for 3 minutes.

2 Add the garlic, sea salt, black pepper, and red pepper, and cook for 3 minutes, or until the pepper has softened.

3 Remove from the heat, stir in the basil, and serve. Makes 4 servings.

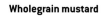

Wholegrain mustard

DAIRY FREE **NUT FREE** **PALEO DIET**

Oven-Roasted Moroccan Chicken

Citrusy lemon and coriander blend with sweet-smelling spices to create a chermoula, a Moroccan marinade that makes this chicken dish so succulent and aromatic.

Prep Time
20 minutes + 4 hours marinating

Cook Time
60 minutes

Makes
4 servings

INGREDIENTS

1 small onion, diced

6 garlic cloves, chopped

250g (9oz) passata

60ml (2fl oz) lemon juice

2 tbsp ghee or animal fat

10g (1/4oz) coriander leaves, chopped

1 tbsp paprika

1 tsp sea salt

1 tsp grated fresh root ginger

1 tsp black pepper

1/2 tsp ground cumin

1/2 tsp ground turmeric

4 skin-on, bone-in chicken leg quarters, about 1kg (2lb) in total

METHOD

1 In a large bowl, whisk together the onion, garlic, passata, lemon juice, ghee, coriander, paprika, sea salt, ginger, black pepper, cumin, and turmeric.

2 Add the chicken leg quarters, and coat with the spice mix marinade. Cover the bowl tightly with foil or cling film, and chill in the fridge for at least 4 hours or overnight. Because the raw chicken has been sitting in the marinade, do not reuse it as a sauce, as this increases the risk of food-borne illness. Instead, double the marinade recipe, and set aside half of it to use it as a condiment.

3 Preheat the oven to 180°C (350°F/Gas 4). Remove the chicken from the marinade, and place skin-side up and evenly spaced apart in a 23 × 33cm (9 × 13inch) baking dish.

4 Roast on the middle oven shelf for 1 hour, or until the chicken is cooked through or it reaches an internal temperature of 75°C (165°F) and the juice runs clear.

Arrange the quarters in a dish for even cooking

Side Dish

Moroccan Cauliflower "Couscous"

FULL DIET

INGREDIENTS

1 head of cauliflower, stemmed,
  cored and grated

4 tbsp ghee or animal fat

25g (scant 1oz) spring onions,
  thinly sliced

3 garlic cloves, crushed

30g (1oz) raisins

30g (1oz) slivered almonds

3 tbsp fresh orange juice

2 tsp orange zest

240ml (8fl oz) home-made
  chicken stock

1 tbsp Ras el Hanout

1 tsp sea salt

1 tsp cider vinegar

METHOD

1 In a medium saucepan over a medium-high heat, combine the ghee or animal fat, spring onions, garlic, raisins, almonds, orange juice, orange zest, chicken stock, grated cauliflower, Ras el Hanout, sea salt, and cider vinegar.

2 Bring to the boil, cover, reduce the heat to medium-low, and simmer for 2 minutes. Uncover, and cook, stirring occasionally, for another 1–2 minutes, or until the liquid has cooked away. Makes 4 servings.

DAIRY FREE

NUT FREE

PALEO DIET

Slammin' Hot Slaw

If you like spice, you'll love this slaw. It's crunchy, citrusy, smoky — and hot. It goes perfectly with grilled fish.

Prep Time
15 minutes

Makes
about 10 servings

INGREDIENTS

180ml (6fl oz) home-made aioli or mayonnaise

2 tbsp raw honey

1 tbsp chipotle powder

2 tbsp cider vinegar

2 tbsp fresh lime juice

$^1/_2$ tsp sea salt

$^1/_4$ tsp ground black pepper

350g (12oz) shredded green cabbage

75g (2$^1/_2$oz) shredded purple cabbage

1 small yellow pepper, ribs and seeds removed, halved and thinly sliced

1 small red pepper, ribs and seeds removed, halved and thinly sliced

100g (3$^1/_2$oz) spring onions, thinly sliced

1 carrot, coarsely grated

10g ($^1/_2$oz) chopped coriander leaves

1 garlic clove, crushed

2 oranges, in segments

150g (5$^1/_2$oz) cherry tomatoes, halved

2 jalapeños, stem removed, thinly sliced

METHOD

1 In a small bowl, whisk together the aioli, honey, chipotle powder, cider vinegar, lime juice, sea salt, and black pepper.

2 In a large bowl, combine the green cabbage, purple cabbage, yellow pepper, red pepper, spring onions, carrots, coriander, garlic, orange segments, cherry tomatoes, and jalapeños.

3 Add the dressing to the cabbage mixture, and toss to combine.

4 Chill, tightly covered, in the fridge for 1 hour before serving.

Q&A

How do I adjust the heat?

To increase the hotness factor of this recipe, substitute habanero or Scotch bonnet peppers for the jalapeños. To tone things down a bit, remove the seeds and ribs from the jalapeños, or substitute a milder chilli, cut back on the chipotle powder amount, or substitute smoked paprika for the chipotle.

Chilli peppers

NUT
FREE

Tiger Prawn and Cauliflower Grits

This American country-style recipe features buttery, cheesy cauliflower beneath rich prawns in a savoury tomato sauce. It's a satisfying dish, great for any meal.

Cauliflower

Prep Time
10 minutes

Cook Time
20 minutes

Makes
4 servings

INGREDIENTS

1 large head of cauliflower, cut into 2.5cm (1in) florets

4 tbsp ghee or animal fat

2 garlic cloves, crushed

$1/2$ small onion, diced

16–20 fresh tiger prawns, peeled, deveined, and tails removed

1 tbsp lemon juice

125g ($4^1/2$oz) passata

$3/4$ tsp sea salt

$1/2$ tsp ground black pepper

1 tbsp chopped oregano leaves

180ml (6fl oz) home-made chicken stock

2 tbsp chopped flat-leaf parsley

80ml ($2^1/2$fl oz) extra virgin olive oil

2 tbsp chopped spring onions, green parts only

50g ($1^3/4$oz) grated Pecorino cheese

METHOD

1 In a large saucepan over a medium-high heat, bring 240ml (8fl oz) of water to the boil. Reduce the heat to medium, place a steamer insert in the pan, and steam the cauliflower florets for 20 minutes.

2 In a large frying pan over a medium heat, heat 2 tablespoons of ghee. Add 1 garlic clove, the onion, and prawns, and cook, stirring regularly, for 3 minutes.

3 Add the lemon juice, passata, $1/4$ teaspoon of sea salt, $1/4$ teaspoon of black pepper, the oregano, and 120ml (4fl oz) of stock. Cook, stirring regularly, for 5 minutes.

4 Remove from the heat, stir in the flat-leaf parsley, cover, and set aside.

5 Drain the cauliflower in a colander and transfer to a food processor fitted with a metal chopping blade. Add the remaining chicken stock, the remaining garlic clove, remaining 2 tablespoons of ghee, remaining $1/2$ teaspoon of sea salt, remaining $1/4$ teaspoon of black pepper, and the olive oil, and process until smooth.

6 Transfer the cauliflower grits to a bowl, stir in the spring onions and Pecorino, and serve with the prawns on top or alongside.

DAIRY
FREE

NUT
FREE

PALEO
DIET

Kimchi

This crispy Asian condiment provides a combination of salty, sweet, spicy, and sour flavours in each gut-nourishing bite. It will quickly become one of your staple recipes.

Prep Time
20 minutes

Cook Time
7 days

Makes
2 1-litre jars, about 30 servings

INGREDIENTS

2 small heads of Chinese leaves, shredded

2 red peppers, ribs and seeds removed, thinly sliced

300g (10oz) radishes or mooli, thinly sliced

4 carrots, grated

50g (1¾oz) grated fresh root ginger

6 garlic cloves, thinly sliced

4 spring onions, thinly sliced

2 tsp Korean fish sauce, GAPS legal, no sugar added

3 tbsp sea salt

spring or filtered water

METHOD

1 In a large bowl, combine the Chinese leaves, red peppers, radishes or mooli, carrots, ginger, garlic, spring onions, and Korean fish sauce. Add the sea salt, and massage the salt into the vegetables until they soften and liquid brine stops forming.

2 Using a wooden spoon, evenly pack the vegetables and brine into 1-litre glass jars, packing down the vegetables so they're completely submerged, and leaving at least 2.5cm (1in) space at the top of the jar. Add spring water, if necessary, to cover.

3 Cover the jars with lids, and set aside at room temperature, out of direct sunlight, for 7 days.

4 Once daily, loosen the lids to allow the gases to escape. Press down on the vegetables as needed to ensure they remain submerged in the brine. Retighten the lids. Can be stored in the fridge for up to 6 months.

Variation

Kowabunga Kimchi

Add 1 teaspoon of
Korean chilli powder or
crushed dried chillies, or 1 (or more)
chopped red Thai or red jalapeño
chillies to the vegetable mix.

DAIRY FREE

NUT FREE

PALEO DIET

Cauliflower Hummus

This soft, toasted, slightly lemony Mediterranean purée makes a great sandwich spread or dip. This version substitutes cauliflower for the traditional chickpeas. Who says white foods can't be great for you?

Prep Time	**Cook Time**	**Makes**
15 minutes	20 minutes	8 servings

INGREDIENTS

1 large head of cauliflower, outer leaves, tough stems, and core removed, and cut into florets

115g (4oz) tahini paste

60ml (2fl oz) extra virgin olive oil

1 garlic clove

1 tsp ground cumin

2 tbsp lemon juice

1 tsp sea salt

$1/4$ tsp black pepper

METHOD

1 In a large saucepan over a medium-high heat, bring 240ml (8fl oz) of water to the boil.

2 Reduce the heat to medium, and place a steamer insert in the pan. Add the cauliflower, cover, and cook for 20 minutes, or until it is soft and fork-tender. Drain the cauliflower into a colander, and cool completely.

3 In a food processor fitted with a metal chopping blade, process the cooled cauliflower, tahini paste, olive oil, garlic, cumin, lemon juice, sea salt, and black pepper until smooth.

4 Keep tightly covered in the refrigerator until ready to use.

Variation

Roasted Aubergine Spread

FULL DIET

Substitute roasted aubergine for the cauliflower. Preheat the oven to 190°C (375°F/Gas 5), cut 1 large auberine in half lengthways, prick the skin side with a fork, and place skin-side up on a baking sheet. Roast on the middle shelf for 40 minutes, or until the flesh is completely softened. Carefully scrape the roasted flesh from the skin, and allow it to cool completely. Proceed as directed.

Aubergine

DAIRY FREE   NUT FREE   PALEO DIET

Garden Fresh Salsa

Toss together some sweet, ripe tomatoes, citrusy coriander, a burst of lime acidity, a bit of optional chilli heat, and a dash of sea salt, and you have the makings of one of the simplest yet tastiest fresh salsas.

Prep Time
15 minutes

Makes
8 servings

INGREDIENTS

500g (1lb 2oz) tomatoes, deseeded
  and chopped
1 small red onion, finely diced
$^1/_2$ garlic clove, crushed
$^1/_2$ tsp ground cumin
10g ($^1/_4$oz) coriander leaves, chopped
2 tbsp fresh lime juice
$^3/_4$ tsp sea salt
$^1/_4$ tsp ground black pepper
1 tbsp green serrano, jalapeño, or
  poblano chiles, deseeded (optional)

METHOD

1 In a food processor fitted with a metal chopping blade, pulse the tomatoes, red onion, garlic, cumin, coriander, lime juice, sea salt, black pepper, and chillies (if using) until the ingredients are finely chopped and well combined.

2 Transfer to a bowl, cover tightly, and store in the fridge until needed.

NUT FREE

Tzatziki Sauce

Delectably cool and creamy, this dip is quick to make and lends a Greek flavour to dipping crudités. You can also use it to top grilled meat or fish.

Prep Time
15 minutes

Makes
8 servings

INGREDIENTS

500ml (16fl oz) home-made
  yogurt
240g (8oz) cucumber, peeled,
  deseeded, and finely grated
1 garlic clove, crushed
1 tbsp lemon juice
2 tbsp fresh dill weed
1 tsp sea salt
$^1/_4$ tsp ground black pepper

METHOD

1 In a medium bowl, combine the yogurt, cucumber, garlic, lemon juice, dill weed, sea salt, and black pepper.

2 Cover tightly, and chill in the fridge for 1 hour before serving.

NUT
FREE

LOW
FODMAP

Parmesan Rosemary Tuiles

These thin, crisp crackers burst with the fresh flavours of rosemary, lemon, and ground black pepper. You can substitute the herbs and spices as preferred.

Prep Time
10 minutes

Cook Time
5 minutes

Makes
6 servings of 2 tuiles

INGREDIENTS

100g (3¹/₂oz) grated
   Parmesan cheese
1 tbsp rosemary leaves
1 tsp lemon zest
¹/₂ tsp black pepper

METHOD

1 Preheat the oven to 400°F 200°C (400°F/Gas 6). Line a medium baking sheet with baking parchment.

2 In a small bowl, combine the Parmesan, rosemary, lemon zest, and black pepper.

3 Place 1 heaped tablespoon of the cheese mixture onto the baking parchment, gently pressing down to spread. Repeat, separating each cheese circle by 2.5cm (1in), to make a total of 12 tuiles.

4 Bake on the middle oven shelf for 5 minutes, or until the cheese is crisp and golden.

5 Cool completely, remove the tuiles from the tray with a spatula, and rest them on the curve of a rolling pin until bent. Or lay them flat on a separate plate. If not serving immediately, store the tuiles tightly covered at room temperature for up to 1 week.

PALEO DIET

Three-Seed Crackers

When you want something crispy, crunchy, and salty, reach for these tasty crackers. They make an excellent accompaniment to salads.

Prep Time
10 minutes

Cook Time
30 minutes

Makes
6 servings of 5 crackers

INGREDIENTS

115g (4oz) hazelnut flour/meal

115g (4oz) almond flour/meal

2 large free-range eggs

30g (1oz) raw sunflower seeds, soaked and dried

30g (1oz) raw pumpkin seeds, soaked and dried

30g (1oz) raw sesame seeds, soaked and dried

1 tsp garlic powder

1 tsp onion powder

1 tsp sea salt

$^1/_4$ tsp black pepper

METHOD

1 Preheat the oven to 180°C (350°F/Gas 4).

2 In a food processor, combine the hazelnut flour, almond flour, eggs, sunflower seeds, pumpkin seeds, sesame seeds, garlic powder, onion powder, sea salt, and black pepper until well combined in a dough-like texture.

3 Place the dough on one half of a piece of baking parchment. Fold the paper over on top of the dough, and roll into a square with an even thickness of 3mm ($^1/_8$in).

4 Using a blunt knife, cut into 30 squares. Place the squares on a baking sheet lined with baking parchment, and bake on the middle oven shelf for 30 minutes, or until lightly browned, using a spatula to turn the crackers halfway through.

" Seeds add a nutritional boost by contributing helpful fatty acids, amino acids, zinc, selenium, and magnesium. If sunflower, pumpkin, and sesame aren't to your liking, you can substitute 30g (1oz) poppy seeds, 50g (1$^3/_4$oz) hemp seeds, or 45g (1$^1/_2$oz) flaxseeds. "

DAIRY FREE

PALEO DIET

Nut Butter

When properly soaked, dried nuts are easy to turn into delicious nut butter. Far better than anything from the supermarket, this nut butter is packed with healthy fat, protein, and energy.

Prep Time
5 minutes

Cook Time
10 minutes

Makes
about 30 servings of 2 tablespoons

INGREDIENTS

500g (1lb 2oz) soaked and dried nuts
4 tbsp coconut oil, melted
$\frac{1}{8}$ tsp sea salt

METHOD

1 In a food processor fitted with a metal chopping blade, pulse the nuts until they resemble flour.

2 Add the coconut oil and sea salt, and process, stopping to scrape down the sides of the bowl as needed, until the nut butter has reached your desired consistency.

3 Transfer the nut butter to a glass jar, seal tightly, and store in the fridge for up to 6 months.

Variation

Coconut Butter

FULL DIET

Pulse 300g (10oz) unsweetened coconut flakes about 10 times in a food processor fitted with a metal chopping blade, and then process for 10–20 minutes, scraping down the sides of the bowl as necessary. Store in a glass jar at room temperature for up to 6 months.

DAIRY FREE **PALEO DIET**

Nut Cheese

If you have a dairy allergy, nut cheese – which can be spreadable or hard in texture – can be a tasty substitute. Take care, though, because nuts can sometimes be difficult to digest, even when properly prepared.

Prep Time	Makes	Serving Size
15 minutes	about 250g (9oz)	about 5 servings of 3 tablespoons

INGREDIENTS

150g (5$\frac{1}{2}$oz) cashews or almonds, soaked overnight with 1 tsp sea salt, and skins removed (if needed)

180ml (6fl oz) water

2 tbsp coconut oil, melted

3 tsp lemon juice

1 garlic clove

$\frac{1}{8}$ tsp sea salt

METHOD

1 In a blender, process the nuts, water, coconut oil, lemon juice, garlic, and sea salt for 5–7 minutes, or until smooth.

2 Transfer the mixture to a nut milk bag, or a colander lined with cheesecloth, press down on the solids or squeeze to remove the excess liquid, and form the cheese into a ball.

3 Serve immediately, for a creamier cheese. For a harder cheese, chill in the fridge for 24 hours before serving.

DAIRY FREE

PALEO DIET

Spiced Carrot Cake

Fragrant spices, naturally sweet carrots, plump raisins, crunchy walnuts, and a super-moist texture combine to make this cake irresistible.

Prep Time	Cook Time	Makes
15 minutes	45 minutes	16 servings

INGREDIENTS

120ml (4fl oz) raw honey
115g (4oz) coconut oil, softened
5 large free-range eggs
2 tsp pure vanilla extract
400g (14oz) almond flour
1 tsp ground ginger
3 tsp ground cinnamon
$1/2$ tsp ground nutmeg
$1^1/2$ tsp baking soda
$1/2$ tsp sea salt
125g ($4^1/2$ oz) finely grated carrots
75g ($2^1/2$oz) raw walnuts, soaked and dried, chopped
100g ($3^1/2$oz) raisins

METHOD

1 Preheat the oven to 160°C (325°F/Gas 3). Grease a 20 x 20cm (8 x 8in) glass baking dish with 1 teaspoon of coconut oil.

2 With a mixer on a medium setting, cream together the honey and coconut oil. Add the eggs one at a time, and beat until well combined. Add the vanilla extract, and mix until combined.

3 In a separate bowl, combine the almond flour, ginger, cinnamon, nutmeg, baking soda, and sea salt.

4 With the mixer on a low setting, gradually add the dry ingredients to the wet and mix until well combined. Add the carrots, walnuts, and raisins, and mix.

5 Pour into the baking dish, and bake on the middle oven shelf for 45 minutes.

Variation

Courgette Sunflower Cake with Currants

Substitute 150g ($5^1/2$oz) grated courgette for the carrots; 100g ($3^1/2$oz) of raw sunflower seeds for the walnuts; and 100g ($3^1/2$oz) dried currants for the raisins. Proceed as directed.

FULL DIET

Pure vanilla extract

Ground cinnamon

DAIRY FREE   **PALEO DIET**

Hunger Buster Bars

Soft and chewy but substantial, these bars make a great snack between meals or packed in school lunches. Make a double batch to last all week.

Prep Time
15 minutes

Cook Time
15 minutes

Makes
20 bars

INGREDIENTS

75g (2^1/$_2$oz) raw whole almonds, soaked and dried

75g (2^1/$_2$oz) raw whole cashews, soaked and dried

75g (2^1/$_2$oz) raw pumpkin seeds, soaked and dried

75g (2^1/$_2$oz) raw peanuts, soaked and dried

150g (5^1/$_2$oz) unsweetened shredded coconut

75g (2^1/$_2$oz) raw sesame seeds, soaked and dried

75g (2^1/$_2$oz) raw sunflower seeds, soaked and dried

100g (3^1/$_2$oz) hemp seeds, soaked and dried

75g (2^1/$_2$oz) dried figs (no sulphur)

375g (13oz) home-made almond butter

180ml (6fl oz) raw honey

1 tsp pure vanilla extract

METHOD

1 Preheat the oven to 180°C (350°F/Gas 4). Grease a 23 x 33cm (9 x 13in) baking tray with 1 teaspoon of coconut oil.

2 In a food processor fitted with a metal chopping blade, briefly pulse the almonds, cashews, pumpkin seeds, and peanuts until roughly chopped. Transfer to a large bowl.

3 To the bowl, add the coconut, sesame seeds, sunflower seeds, hemp seeds, and figs, and mix to combine.

4 In a small saucepan over a medium heat, melt the almond butter and honey for 3 minutes, whisking frequently. Remove from the heat and stir in the vanilla extract.

5 Pour the almond butter mixture over the nut, seed, and coconut mixture, and stir to combine.

6 Using wet hands, spread the mixture in an even layer on the prepared baking tray, patting it down into a 2.5cm (1in) thick rectangle. Bake on the middle oven shelf for 15 minutes. Cool completely before cutting. Store tightly covered in a cool, dry place for up to 1 week.

" These bars are a breeze to customize. Instead of the almond butter, try peanut butter, tahini paste, cashew butter, or sunflower butter. In place of the figs, you could use raisins, dried apples, currants, apricots, or peaches. Feeling spicy? Add ground cinnamon or ginger. "

DAIRY FREE **NUT FREE** **PALEO DIET**

Very Berry "Ice Cream"

Creamy and delicate, this nutritionally enhanced version of the classic dessert is just as delicious.

Prep Time
15 minutes + 2 hours

Makes
8 servings

INGREDIENTS

2 ripe bananas, peeled, cut into thin rounds, and frozen overnight

250g (9oz) fresh or 500g (1lb 2oz) frozen strawberries, blueberries, raspberries, and/or blackberries (frozen overnight if fresh)

1 tbsp raw honey

METHOD

1 In a food processor fitted with a metal chopping blade, pulse the frozen bananas and berries, stopping to scrape down the sides of the food processor bowl as needed, until a creamy texture is reached.

2 Add the honey, and process to combine.

3 Transfer the ice cream to an airtight container, cover, and place in the freezer for 2 hours, or until frozen.

DAIRY FREE

Lemon Almond Flour Biscotti

These crunchy, twice-baked bites of semi-sweet goodness have a hint of lemon flavour, and the nuttiness of whole chopped almonds.

Prep Time
10 minutes

Cook Time
40 minutes

Makes
20 servings of 2 biscotti

INGREDIENTS

2 large eggs
60ml (2fl oz) raw honey
60g (2oz) coconut oil
2 tbsp lemon zest
2 tbsp lemon juice
350g (12oz) almond flour
115g (4oz) hazelnut flour
60g (2oz) flaxseed meal
60g (2oz) slivered
   almonds, chopped
1 tsp sea salt
2 tsp baking soda
$1^1/_2$ tsp ground cinnamon

METHOD

1 Preheat the oven to 160°C (325°F/Gas 3). Line a 46 x 33cm (18 x 13in) baking sheet with baking parchment.

2 In a medium bowl, whisk together the eggs, honey, coconut oil, lemon zest, and lemon juice.

3 In another medium bowl, combine the almond flour, hazelnut flour, flaxseed meal, slivered almonds, sea salt, baking soda, and cinnamon. Stir the wet ingredients into the dry ingredients until well combined.

4 Place the biscotti dough on a piece of baking parchment, and form into a log 39cm ($15^1/_2$in) long and 3.75cm ($1^1/_2$in) in diameter.

5 Bake on the middle oven shelf for 20 minutes, or until the top is just browning. Allow to rest for 5 minutes. If the log has cracked, carefully squeeze it together.

6 Using a sharp chef's knife or serrated knife, cut the log into 1.25cm ($^1/_2$-inch) thick diagonal pieces. Place the cut pieces flat in a single layer on the baking parchment, and bake for another 20 minutes, turning the biscotti halfway through. Let them cool completely before serving.

Index of Recipes by Type

DAIRY FREE

Apple Pie Stewed Apples, 154
Aromatic Chicken with Mushrooms, 126
Asian Braised Turkey Meatballs, 110
Asparagus Fried Eggs, 122
Baked Cinnamon Walnut Apples, 155
Beef Bone Broth, 60
Beetroot and Beef Short Rib
    Borscht, 98
Braised Beef Burgers, 108
Braised Tomato Sage Turkey Legs, 116
Butternut Squash Soup, 85
Carrot Beet Soup, 86
Cauliflower Hummus, 202
Chicken Enchilada Casserole, 114
Chicken Muffins, 131
Chicken Stock, 59
Chicken-Stuffed Cabbage Rolls, 111
Chicken Vegetable Ratatouille, 112
Chicken Vegetable Soup, 88
Chopped Cobb Salad, 178
Chunky Chicken Salad, 188
Classic Chicken Soup, 84
Classic Pot Roast with Onions, 139
Crackling Nuts, 143
Cultured Spring Vegetables, 67
Dairy-Free Key Lime Mousse, 164
Easy Avocado Omelette, 125
Easy Chicken Stir-Fry, 151
Egg Drop Soup, 106
Everyday Grain-Free Bread, 78
Fermented Mixed Vegetables, 66
Garden Fresh Salsa, 203
Garlic Chicken with Vegetables, 134
Garlicky Greens Soup, 89
Ginger Pumpkin Muffins, 130
Gingered Vanilla Honey Drops, 169
Grain-Free Tabbouleh, 147
Grainless Granola, 176

Greek Lemon Vegetable Soup, 97
Green Goddess Juice, 132
Grilled Vegetable Frittata, 177
Guacamole, 150
Honey Dombs, 168
Honey Sage Sausage Patties, 172
Hunger Buster Bars, 211
Kimchi, 200
Lamb Burger Sliders, 192
Lemon Peppercorn Poached Chicken
    Breast, 101
Lemon Almond Flour Biscotti, 214
Lemon Rosemary Salmon, 115
Liver-Loving Juice, 133
Meat Stock, 58
Minced Beef Empanadas, 142
Mini Butternut Squash Soufflés, 148
Nut Butter, 208
Nut Cheese, 209
Nut Milk, 71
Olive Raisin Tapenade, 162
Oven-Roasted Moroccan Chicken, 196
Oven-Roasted Turkey Meatloaf, 138
Pan Steak with Mushrooms, 102
Peppery Pear Juice, 132
Red Cabbage Kraut, 64
Roasted Butternut Squash
    Pancakes, 124
Salmon Spinach Cobb Salad, 186
Sauerkraut Scramble, 120
Seared Scallop Salad with Asian
    Vegetables, 182
Seasonal Mixed-Berry Crostata, 166
Simple House Salad, 146
Slammin' Hot Slaw, 198
"Spaghetti" with Pomodoro Sauce, 136
Spiced Carrot Cake, 210
Spring Tuna Niçoise Salad, 185
Summer Garden Soup, 92
Sweet-and-Sour Chicken Vegetable
    Soup, 90
Tex-Mex Pulled Pork Burritos, 152

LOW FODMAP

Three-Onion Soup, 93
Tuna Cakes with Rémoulade, 195
Vegetable Beef Stewp, 107
Very Berry "Ice Cream", 212
Beetroot and Beef Short Rib
    Borscht, 98
Ghee, 70
Grilled Salmon with Walnut Pesto, 135
Home-Churned Butter, 68
Parmesan Rosemary Tuiles, 204
Red Cabbage Kraut, 64
Simple House Salad, 146
Stewed Beef Porridge, 100

NUT FREE

Apple Pie Stewed Apples, 154
Aromatic Chicken with Mushrooms, 126
Asian Braised Turkey Meatballs, 110
Beef Bone Broth, 60
Beetroot and Beef Short Rib
    Borscht, 98
Braised Beef Burgers, 108
Braised Tomato Sage Turkey Legs, 116
Butternut Squash Soup, 85
Carrot Beetroot Soup, 86
Cauliflower Hummus, 202
Chicken Cheddar Sandwiches, 190
Chicken Enchilada Casserole, 114
Chicken Stock, 59
Chicken-Stuffed Cabbage Rolls, 111
Chicken Thigh Puttanesca, 163
Chicken Vegetable Ratatouille, 112
Chicken Vegetable Soup, 88
Chopped Cobb Salad, 178
Classic Chicken Soup, 84

Classic Pot Roast with Onions, 139
Creamy Tomato Soup, 96
Cultured Spring Vegetables, 67
Easy Avocado Omelette, 125
Easy Chicken Stir-Fry, 151
Egg Drop Soup, 106
Fermented Mixed Vegetables, 66
Garden Fresh Salsa, 203
Garlic Chicken with Vegetables, 134
Garlicky Greens Soup, 89
Ghee, 70
Gingered Vanilla Honey Drops, 169
Grain-Free Tabbouleh, 147
Greek Lemon Vegetable Soup, 97
Green Goddess Juice, 132
Grilled Steak Salad, 181
Grilled Vegetable Frittata, 177
Guacamole, 150
Home-Churned Butter, 68
Honey Bombs, 168
Honey Sage Sausage Patties, 172
Kefir, 77
Kimchi, 200
Lemon Peppercorn Poached Chicken
    Breast, 101
Lemon Rosemary Salmon, 115
Liver-Loving Juice, 133
Margherita Pizza, 194
Meat Stock, 58
Minced Beef Stroganoff, 140
Mini Butternut Squash Soufflés, 148
Olive Raisin Tapenade, 162
Oven-Roasted Moroccan Chicken,
    196
Pan Steak with Mushrooms, 102
Parmesan Rosemary Tuiles, 204
Peppery Pear Juice, 132
Pumpkin Bisque, 94
Santa Fe Breakfast Tostadas, 121
Sauerkraut Scramble, 120
Sausage, Egg, and Cheese
    Sandwich, 173
Scallops Piccata, 160
Seared Scallop Salad with Asian
    Vegetables, 182
Simple House Salad, 146
Skillet Asparagus and Eggs, 122
Slammin' Hot Slaw, 198

"Spaghetti" with Pomodoro Sauce,
    136
Stewed Beef Porridge, 100
Summer Garden Soup, 92
Sweet-and-Sour Chicken Vegetable
    Soup, 90
Three-Onion Soup, 93
Tiger Prawn and Cauliflower Grits, 199
Tzatziki Sauce, 203
Vegetable Beef Stewp, 107
Very Berry "Ice Cream," 212
Wedge Salad with Ranch, 184
Yogurt, 74

PALEO DIET

Apple Pie Stewed Apples, 154
Aromatic Chicken with Mushrooms, 126
Asian Braised Turkey Meatballs, 110
Asparagus Fried Eggs, 122
Beef Bone Broth, 60
Beetroot and Beef Short Rib
    Borscht, 98
Braised Beef Burgers, 108
Braised Tomato Sage Turkey Legs, 116
Butternut Squash Soup, 85
Carrot Beetroot Soup, 86
Cauliflower Hummus, 202
Chicken Enchilada Casserole, 114
Chicken Muffins, 131
Chicken Stock, 59
Chicken-Stuffed Cabbage Rolls, 111
Chicken Thigh Puttanesca, 163
Chicken Vegetable Ratatouille, 112
Chopped Cobb Salad, 178
Chunky Chicken Salad, 188
Classic Chicken Soup, 84
Classic Pot Roast with Onions, 139
Crackling Nuts, 143
Creamy Tomato Soup, 96
Cultured Spring Vegetables, 67
Dairy-Free Key Lime Mousse, 166
Easy Avocado Omelet, 125
Easy Chicken Stir-Fry, 151
Egg Drop Soup, 106
Everyday Grain-Free Bread, 78

Fermented Mixed Vegetables, 66
Garden Fresh Salsa, 203
Garlic Chicken with Vegetables, 134
Garlicky Greens Soup, 89
Ginger Pumpkin Muffins, 130
Gingered Vanilla Honey Drops, 169
Grain-Free Tabbouleh, 147
Grainless Granola, 176
Greek Lemon Vegetable Soup, 97
Green Goddess Juice, 132
Grilled Salmon with Walnut
    Pesto, 135
Grilled Vegetable Frittata, 177
Guacamole, 150
Hunger Buster Bars, 211
Kimchi, 200
Lemon Rosemary Salmon, 115
Liver-Loving Juice, 133
Meat Stock, 58
Minced Beef Empanadas, 142
Nut Butter, 208
Nut Cheese, 209
Nut Milk, 71
Oven-Roasted Moroccan Chicken,
    196
Oven-Roasted Turkey Meatloaf, 138
Pan Steak with Mushrooms, 102
Peppery Pear Juice, 132
Salmon Spinach Cobb Salad, 186
Santa Fe Breakfast Tostadas, 121
Sauerkraut Scramble, 120
Seared Scallop Salad with Asian
    Vegetables, 182
Seasonal Mixed-Berry Crostata, 166
Simple House Salad, 146
Slammin' Hot Slaw, 198
"Spaghetti" with Pomodoro Sauce, 136
Spiced Carrot Cake, 210
Stewed Beef Porridge, 100
Summer Garden Soup, 92
Sweet-and-Sour Chicken Vegetable
    Soup, 90
Tex-Mex Pulled Pork Burritos, 152
Three-Onion Soup, 93
Three-Seed Crackers, 206
Vegetable Beef Stewp, 107
Very Berry "Ice Cream," 212

Index

A

alcohol, 51
almonds
Almond Butter Honey Spread, 124
Almond Flour Wraps, 153
Almond Milk Yogurt, 75
Anytime Smoothie, 158
apples
Apple Pie Stewed Apples, 154
Baked Cinnamon Walnut Apples, 155
Chamomile Ginger Apple Sauce, 154
Roasted Brussels Sprout Apple Salad, 159
Aromatic Chicken with Mushrooms, 126
Asian Braised Turkey Meatballs, 110
asparagus
Grilled Steak and Asparagus with Poached Eggs, 123
Asparagus Fried Eggs, 122
avocados
Avocado Enchiladas, 114
Dairy-Free Key Lime Mousse, 166
Dairy-Free Raspberry Avocado Mousse, 167
Easy Avocado Omelette, 125
Guacamole, 150
Pesto Guacamole, 150
Salmon, Spinach, and Tomato Omelette with Avocado, 125
Sun-Dried Guacamole, 150

B

Baked Apples with Cinnamon, Walnuts, Raisins, and Yogurt, 155
Baked Cinnamon Walnut Apples, 155
bananas
Dairy-Free Key Lime Mousse, 166
Dairy-Free Raspberry Avocado Mousse, 167
beef
Beef Bone Broth, 60
Beetroot and Beef Short Rib Borscht, 98
Braised Beef Burgers, 108
Classic Pot Roast with Onions, 139
Grilled Steak and Asparagus with Poached Eggs, 123
Grilled Steak Salad, 181
Meat Stock, 58
Minced Beef Empanadas, 142
Minced Beef Stroganoff, 140
Pan Steak with Mushrooms, 102
Philly Cheesesteak Pizza, 194
Slow Cooker Beetroot and Beef Short Rib Borscht, 99
Slow Cooker Pot Roast with Onions, 139

Stewed Beef Porridge, 100
Sweet-and-Sour Beef Vegetable Soup, 91
Three-Onion Soup, 93
Vegetable Beef Stewp, 107
beetroot
Beetroot and Beef Short Rib Borscht, 98
Carrot Beetroot Soup, 86
Liver-Loving Juice, 133
body preparations, 20
brain digestion functions, 10
Braised Beef Burgers, 108
Braised Tomato Sage Turkey Legs, 116
breads
Almond Flour Wraps, 153
Cheddar Chive Biscuits, 174
Everyday Grain-Free Bread, 78
breakfast
Cheddar Chive Biscuits, 174
Easy Avocado Omelette, 125
Ginger Pumpkin Muffins, 130
Grainless Granola, 176
Grilled Steak and Asparagus with Poached Eggs, 123
Grilled Vegetable Frittata, 177
Honey Sage Sausage Patties, 172
Italian Sausage Egg Sandwich, 173
Mini Butternut Squash Soufflés, 148
Roasted Vegetable Frittata, 177
Roasted Butternut Squash Pancakes, 124
Salmon, Spinach, and Tomato Omelette with Avocado, 125
sample meal plans
full diet, 52–53
Stage 1, 28–29
Stage 2, 32–33
Stage 3, 36–37
Stage 4, 40–41
Stage 5, 44–45
Stage 6, 48–49
Santa Fe Breakfast Tostadas, 121
Sauerkraut Scramble, 120
Sausage, Egg, and Cheese Sandwich, 173
Sausage Gravy, 175
Spicy Italian Chicken Sausage Patties, 172
broths, 14
Beef Bone Broth, 60
Chicken Bone Broth, 61
Stage 3, 35
storing, 25
butter, 68, 73
butternut squash
Butternut Squash Gnocchi, 141
Butternut Squash Purée, 149
Butternut Squash Soup, 85
Chunky Butternut Kale Soup, 85

Mini Butternut Squash Soufflés, 148
Roasted Butternut Squash Pancakes, 124

C

cabbage
Chicken-Stuffed Cabbage Rolls, 111
Creamy Coleslaw, 190
Cultured Spring Vegetables, 67
Kimchi, 200
Kowabunga Kimchi, 201
Red Cabbage Kraut, 64
Simple Sauerkraut, 62–63
Slammin' Hot Slaw, 198
Sweet-and-Sour Red Slaw, 65
Calming Kale Salad, 180
carrots
Carrot Beetroot Soup, 86
Spiced Carrot Cake, 210
cauliflower
Cauliflower Hummus, 202
Cauliflower Mash, 103
Grain-Free Tabbouleh, 147
grated florets
Greek Lemon Vegetable Soup, 97
Lemon Chicken "Rice" Soup, 84
Lemon Vegetable "Rice" Soup, 97
Moroccan Cauliflower "Couscous", 197
Tiger Prawn and Cauliflower Grits, 199
Chamomile Ginger Apple Sauce, 154
Cheddar Chive Biscuits, 174
Cherry Almond Chiller, 158
Cherry Crostata, 167
chicken
breakfast
Italian Sausage Egg Sandwich, 173
Santa Fe Breakfast Tostadas, 121
Spicy Italian Chicken Sausage Patties, 172
broths/stocks
Chicken Bone Broth, 61
Chicken Stock, 59
Roasted Chicken Stock, 59
cooking internal temperature, 113
main dishes
Aromatic Chicken with Mushrooms, 126
Calming Kale Salad, 180
Chicken Cheddar Sandwiches, 190
Chicken Enchilada Casserole, 114
Chicken Muffins, 131
Chicken-Stuffed Cabbage Rolls, 111
Chicken Thigh Puttanesca, 163
Chicken Vegetable Ratatouille, 112
Chopped Cobb Salad, 178
Chunky Chicken Salad, 188
Easy Chicken Stir-Fry, 151
Garlic Chicken with Vegetables, 134
Lemon Peppercorn Poached Chicken Breast, 101
Oven-Roasted Moroccan Chicken, 196
Spicy Chicken Enchilada Casserole, 114
soups

Chicken Vegetable Soup, 88
Classic Chicken Soup, 84
Greek Lemon Vegetable Soup, 97
Lemon Chicken "Rice" Soup, 84
Lemon Vegetable "Rice" Soup, 97
Sweet-and-Sour Chicken Vegetable Soup, 90
Chocolate Honey Bombs, 168
Chopped Cobb Salad, 178
Chunky Butternut Kale Soup, 85
Chunky Chicken Salad, 188
Classic Chicken Soup, 84
Classic Pot Roast with Onions, 139
coconuts
Coconut Butter, 208
Coconut Milk, 71
Coconut Milk Kefir, 77
Coconut Milk Yogurt, 75
flour, 79, 168
Honey Bombs, 168
cod liver oil, 31
cold-pressed olive oil, 39
condiments
Almond Butter Honey Spread, 124
Cauliflower Hummus, 202
Coconut Butter, 208
Crème Fraîche, 76
Cultured Butter, 76
Cultured Cream, 76
Cumin Mint Aioli, 193
Garden Fresh Salsa, 203
Guacamole, 150
Home-Churned Butter, 68
Honey Mustard Vinaigrette, 187
Horsey Dressing, 181
Nut Butter, 208
Nut Cheese, 209
Olive Raisin Tapenade, 162
Pesto Guacamole, 150
Roasted Aubergine Spread, 202
Russian Dressing, 191
Sun-Dried Guacamole, 150
Tzatziki Sauce, 203
constipation, 18
cooking in advance, 22, 24
courgettes
Courgette Sunflower Cake with Currants, 210
"Spaghetti" with Pomodoro Sauce, 136
crackers
Parmesan Rosemary Tuiles, 204
Three-Seed Crackers, 206
Crackling Nuts, 143
Crackling Seeds, 143
cramps, 18
Creamy Coleslaw, 190
Creamy Tomato Soup, 96
Crème Fraîche, 76
Cultured Butter, 76
Cultured Cream, 76
Cultured Rainbow Vegetables, 67
Cultured Root Vegetables, 67
Cultured Spring Vegetables, 67
culturing
dairy, 15, 27, 72–73
vegetables, 63
Cumin Mint Aioli, 193

D

dairy
butter, 73
cream, 73
cultured, 15, 27, 72–73
full diet, 51
raw milk, 73
recipes
Almond Milk Yogurt, 75
Coconut Milk Kefir, 77
Coconut Milk Yogurt, 75
Crème Fraîche, 76
Cultured Butter, 76
Cultured Cream, 76
Cultured Dairy, 72–73
Flavoured Kefir, 77
Home-Churned Butter, 68
Kefir, 72, 77
Yogurt, 74
reintroducing, 55
Stage 2, 31
sterilization, 72
yogurt, 73
Dairy-Free Key Lime Mousse, 164
Dairy-Free Raspberry Avocado Mousse, 167
dairy-free recipes
Apple Pie Stewed Apples, 154
Aromatic Chicken with Mushrooms, 126
Asian Braised Turkey Meatballs, 110
Asparagus Fried Eggs, 122
Baked Cinnamon Walnut Apples, 155
Beef Bone Broth, 60
Beetroot and Beef Short Rib Borscht, 98
Braised Beef Burgers, 108
Braised Tomato Sage Turkey Legs, 116
Butternut Squash Soup, 85
Carrot Beetroot Soup, 86
Cauliflower Hummus, 202
Chicken Enchilada Casserole, 114
Chicken Muffins, 131
Chicken Stock, 59
Chicken-Stuffed Cabbage Rolls, 111
Chicken Vegetable Ratatouille, 112
Chicken Vegetable Soup, 88
Chopped Cobb Salad, 178
Chunky Chicken Salad, 188
Classic Chicken Soup, 84
Classic Pot Roast with Onions, 139
Crackling Nuts, 143
Cultured Spring Vegetables, 67
Dairy-Free Key Lime Mousse, 164
Easy Avocado Omelette, 125
Easy Chicken Stir-Fry, 151
Egg Drop Soup, 106
Everyday Grain-Free Bread, 78
Fermented Mixed Vegetables, 66
Garden Fresh Salsa, 203
Garlic Chicken with Vegetables, 134
Garlicky Greens Soup, 89
Ginger Pumpkin Muffins, 130
Gingered Vanilla Honey Drops, 169
Grain-Free Tabbouleh, 147
Grainless Granola, 176
Green Goddess Juice, 132

Grilled Vegetable Frittata, 177
Guacamole, 150
Honey Bombs, 168
Honey Sage Sausage Patties, 172
Hunger Buster Bars, 211
Kimchi, 200
Lamb Burger Sliders, 192
Lemon Peppercorn Poached Chicken Breast, 101
Lemon Almond Flour Biscotti, 214
Lemon Rosemary Salmon, 115
Liver-Loving Juice, 133
Meat Stock, 58
Minced Beef Empanadas, 142
Mini Butternut Squash Soufflés, 148
Nut Butter, 208
Nut Cheese, 209
Nut Milk, 71
Olive Raisin Tapenade, 162
Oven-Roasted Moroccan Chicken, 196
Oven-Roasted Turkey Meatloaf, 138
Pan Steak with Mushrooms, 102
Red Cabbage Kraut, 64
Roasted Butternut Squash Pancakes, 124
Salmon Spinach Cobb Salad, 186
Sauerkraut Scramble, 120
Seared Scallop Salad with Asian Vegetables, 182
Seasonal Mixed-Berry Crostata, 166
Simple House Salad, 146
Slammin' Hot Slaw, 198
"Spaghetti" with Pomodoro Sauce, 136
Spiced Carrot Cake, 210
Spring Tuna Niçoise Salad, 185
Summer Garden Soup, 92
Sweet-and-Sour Chicken Vegetable Soup, 90
Tex-Mex Pulled Pork Burritos, 152
Three-Onion Soup, 93
Tuna Cakes with Rémoulade, 195
Vegetable Beef Stewp, 107
Very Berry "Ice Cream," 212
desserts
Apple Pie Stewed Apples, 154
Baked Apples with Cinnamon, Walnuts, Raisins, and Yogurt, 155
Baked Cinnamon Walnut Apples, 155
Chamomile Ginger Apple Sauce, 154
Cherry Crostata, 167
Chocolate Honey Bombs, 168
Courgette Sunflower Cake with Currants, 210
Dairy-Free Key Lime Mousse, 166
Dairy-Free Raspberry Avocado Mousse, 167
Gingered Vanilla Honey Drops, 169
Honey Bombs, 168
Lemon Almond Flour Biscotti, 214
Seasonal Mixed-Berry Crostata, 166
Spiced Carrot Cake, 210
Very Berry "Ice Cream", 212
detox baths, 19
diarrhoea, 18
die-off, 18, 26, 30
digestion problems, 10–11

digestive bitters, 12
digestive enzymes, 12
dips. See condiments
dos and don'ts on the diet, 19
drinks
Anytime Smoothie, 158
Cherry Almond Chiller, 158
Coconut Milk, 71
Flavoured Nut Milk, 71
Golden Goddess Juice, 133
Green Goddess Juice, 132
Liver-Loving Juice, 133
Nut Milk, 71
PB&J Smoothie, 158
Peppery Pear Juice, 132
tea, 27

E

Easy Avocado Omelette, 125
Easy Chicken Stir-Fry, 151
eating out, 19, 38
eggs
Asparagus Fried Eggs, 122
Chopped Cobb Salad, 178
Easy Avocado Omelette, 125
Egg Drop Soup, 106
Grilled Vegetable Frittata, 177
hard-boiling, 178
Italian Sausage Egg Sandwich, 173
Mini Butternut Squash Soufflés, 148
Roasted Vegetable Frittata, 177
Salmon, Spinach, and Tomato Omelette with Avocado, 125
Santa Fe Breakfast Tostadas, 121
Sauerkraut Scramble, 120
Sausage, Egg, and Cheese Sandwich, 173
Stage 3, 35
eliminating foods, 26
emotional expectations, 18
equipment, 22–23
Everyday Grain-Free Bread, 78
expectations, 18
full diet, 50
Stage 1, 26
Stage 2, 30–31
Stage 3, 34
Stage 4, 38
Stage 5, 42
Stage 6, 46

F

fats. See healthy fats
Fermented Mixed Vegetables, 66
fermenting
fruits, 63
vegetables, 15, 35, 62–63
Fish Stock, 59
five R's of gut healing, 12–13
Flavoured Kefir, 77
Flavoured Nut Milk, 71
foods
full diet, 51
journalling, 21
sensitivity testing, 55
Stage 1, 27

Stage 2, 31
Stage 3, 35
Stage 4, 39
Stage 5, 43
Stage 6, 47
storing, 25
sweetened, 47
testing for intolerance, 54
foundation recipes
Almond Milk Yogurt, 75
Beef Bone Broth, 60
Chicken Bone Broth, 61
Chicken Stock, 59
Coconut Milk, 71
Coconut Milk Kefir, 77
Coconut Milk Yogurt, 75
Crème Fraîche, 76
Cultured Butter, 76
Cultured Cream, 76
Cultured Rainbow Vegetables, 67
Cultured Root Vegetables, 67
Cultured Spring Vegetables, 67
Everyday Grain-Free Bread, 78
Fermented Mixed Vegetables, 66
Fish Stock, 59
Flavoured Kefir, 77
Flavoured Nut Milk, 71
Ghee, 70
Home-Churned Butter, 68
Home-Made Coconut Flour, 79
Kefir, 77
Meat Stock, 58
Nut Milk, 71
Red Cabbage Kraut, 64
Roasted Chicken Stock, 59
Sweet-and-Sour Red Slaw, 65
Yogurt, 74
frittatas, 177
fruit
Anytime Smoothie, 158
Apple Pie Stewed Apples, 154
Avocado Enchiladas, 114
Baked Apples with Cinnamon, Walnuts, Raisins, and Yogurt, 155
Baked Cinnamon Walnut Apples, 155
Chamomile Ginger Apple Sauce, 154
Cherry Almond Chiller, 158
Cherry Crostata, 167
Courgette Sunflower Cake with Currants, 210
Dairy-Free Key Lime Mousse, 166
Dairy-Free Raspberry Avocado Mousse, 167
Easy Avocado Omelette, 125
fermenting, 63
Flavoured Kefir, 77
full diet, 51
Ginger Pumpkin Muffins, 130
Golden Goddess Juice, 133
Green Goddess Juice, 132
juices, 43
Liver-Loving Juice, 133
Olive Raisin Tapenade, 162
PB&J Smoothie, 158
Peppery Pear Juice, 132
Pumpkin Bisque, 94
Roasted Pumpkin Bisque, 95

Seasonal Mixed-Berry Crostata, 166
Stage 6, 47
Very Berry "Ice Cream", 212
full diet
    expectations, 50
    recipes
        Beef Bone Broth, 60
        Butternut Squash Gnocchi, 141
        Calming Kale Salad, 180
        Cauliflower Hummus, 202
        Cheddar Chive Biscuits, 174
        Chicken Bone Broth, 61
        Chicken Cheddar Sandwiches, 190
        Chopped Cobb Salad, 178
        Chunky Chicken Salad, 188
        Coconut Butter, 208
        Courgette Sunflower Cake with Currants, 210
        Creamy Coleslaw, 190
        Cumin Mint Aioli, 193
        Flavoured Nut Milk, 71
        Garden Fresh Salsa, 203
        Grainless Granola, 176
        Grilled Steak Salad, 181
        Grilled Vegetable Frittata, 177
        Honey Mustard Vinaigrette, 187
        Honey Sage Sausage Patties, 172
        Horsey Dressing, 181
        Hunger Buster Bars, 211
        Italian Sausage Egg Sandwich, 173
        Kimchi, 200
        Kowabunga Kimchi, 201
        Lamb Burger Sliders, 192
        Lemon Almond Flour Biscotti, 214
        Margherita Pizza, 194
        Moroccan Cauliflower "Couscous", 197
        Nut Butter, 208
        Nut Cheese, 209
        Oven-Roasted Moroccan Chicken, 196
        Parmesan Rosemary Tuiles, 204
        Philly Cheesesteak Pizza, 194
        Roasted Aubergine Spread, 202
        Roasted Vegetable Frittata, 177
        Russian Dressing, 191
        Salmon Spinach Cobb Salad, 186
        Sausage, Egg, and Cheese Sandwich, 173
        Seared Scallop Salad with Asian Vegetables, 182
        Slammin' Hot Slaw, 198
        Spiced Carrot Cake, 210
        Spicy Italian Chicken Sausage Patties, 172
        Spinach Pesto Sauce, 137
        Spring Tuna Niçoise Salad, 185
        Three-Seed Crackers, 206
        Tuna Cakes with Rémoulade, 195
        Turkey Reubens, 191
        Tzatziki Sauce, 203
        Very Berry "Ice Cream", 212
        Warm Portobello, Red Pepper, and Basil Salad, 195
        Wedge Salad with Ranch, 184
    sample meal plan, 52–53
    what you can eat, 51

G
Garden Fresh Salsa, 203
Garden Salad, 146
Garlic Chicken with Vegetables, 134
Garlicky Greens Soup, 89
gas, 18
gelatine, 13
Ghee, 70
Ginger Pumpkin Muffins, 130
Gingered Vanilla Honey Drops, 169
Golden Goddess Juice, 133
Grain-Free Tabbouleh, 147
Grainless Granola, 176
Greek Lemon Vegetable Soup, 97
Green Goddess Juice, 132
greens
    Calming Kale Salad, 180
    Chopped Cobb Salad, 178
    Garden Salad, 146
    Garlicky Greens Soup, 89
    Grain-Free Tabbouleh, 147
    Green Goddess Juice, 132
    Grilled Steak Salad, 181
    Salmon, Spinach, and Tomato Omelette with Avocado, 125
    Seared Scallop Salad with Asian Vegetables, 182
    Simple House Salad, 146
    Spinach Pesto Sauce, 137
    Wedge Salad with Ranch, 184
Grilled Salmon with Walnut Pesto, 135
Grilled Steak and Asparagus with Poached Eggs, 123
Grilled Steak Salad, 181
Grilled Vegetable Frittata, 177
Guacamole, 150

H–I
healthy fats, 14, 24
    Stage 1, 27
    Stage 2, 31
    Stage 3, 35
    Stage 4, 39
Home-Churned Butter, 68
Home-Made Coconut Flour, 79
Home-Made Passata, 163
honey
    Chocolate Honey Bombs, 168
    Gingered Vanilla Honey Drops, 169
    Honey Bombs, 168
    Honey Mustard Vinaigrette, 187
    Honey Sage Sausage Patties, 172
    raw, 169
Horsey Dressing, 181
Hunger Buster Bars, 211

Italian Sausage Egg Sandwich, 173

J–K
journalling, 21
juices
    Golden Goddess Juice, 133
    Green Goddess Juice, 132
    Liver-Loving Juice, 133
    Peppery Pear Juice, 132

kale
    Calming Kale Salad, 180
    Chunky Butternut Kale Soup, 85
Kefir, 72, 77
Kimchi, 200
Kowabunga Kimchi, 201

L
lamb
    Lamb Burger Sliders, 192
    Meat Stock, 58
large intestines, 11, 18
leaky gut syndrome, 10–11
lemon
    Greek Lemon Vegetable Soup, 97
    Lemon Almond Flour Biscotti, 214
    Lemon and Rosemary Butter-Poached Salmon, 115
    Lemon Chicken "Rice" Soup, 84
    Lemon Peppercorn Poached Chicken Breast, 101
    Lemon Rosemary Salmon, 115
    Lemon Vegetable "Rice" Soup, 97
Liver-Loving Juice, 133
local ingredients, finding, 24
low-FODMAP recipes
    Beetroot and Beef Short Rib Borscht, 98
    Garden Salad, 146
    Ghee, 70
    Grilled Salmon with Walnut Pesto, 135
    Home-Churned Butter, 68
    Parmesan Rosemary Tuiles, 204
    Red Cabbage Kraut, 64
    Simple House Salad, 146
    Stewed Beef Porridge, 100
    Sweet-and-Sour Red Slaw, 65
lunch ideas
    full diet, 52–53
    Stage 1, 28–29
    Stage 2, 32–33
    Stage 3, 36–37
    Stage 4, 40–41
    Stage 5, 44–45
    Stage 6, 48–49

M
main dishes
    beef
        Beetroot and Beef Short Rib Borscht, 98
        Braised Beef Burgers, 108
        Classic Pot Roast with Onions, 139
        Minced Beef Empanadas, 142
        Minced Beef Stroganoff, 140
        Pan Steak with Mushrooms, 102
        Philly Cheesesteak Pizza, 194
        Slow Cooker Pot Roast with Onions, 139
    chicken
        Aromatic Chicken with Mushrooms, 126
        Calming Kale Salad, 180
        Chicken Cheddar Sandwiches, 190
        Chicken Enchilada Casserole, 114
        Chicken Muffins, 131

Chicken-Stuffed Cabbage Rolls, 111
        Chicken Thigh Puttanesca, 163
        Chicken Vegetable Ratatouille, 112
        Chopped Cobb Salad, 178
        Chunky Chicken Salad, 188
        Easy Chicken Stir-Fry, 151
        Garlic Chicken with Vegetables, 134
        Lemon Peppercorn Poached Chicken Breast, 101
        Oven-Roasted Moroccan Chicken, 196
        Spicy Chicken Enchilada Casserole, 114
    full diet, 52–53
    Lamb Burger Sliders, 192
    salads
        Calming Kale Salad, 180
        Chopped Cobb Salad, 178
        Chunky Chicken Salad, 188
        Garden Salad, 146
        Grain-Free Tabbouleh, 147
        Grilled Steak Salad, 181
        Seared Scallop Salad with Asian Vegetables, 182
        Simple House Salad, 146
        Spring Tuna Niçoise Salad, 185
        Thai Tuna Salad, 189
        Wedge Salad with Ranch, 184
    seafood
        Grilled Salmon with Walnut Pesto, 135
        Lemon and Rosemary Butter-Poached Salmon, 115
        Scallops Piccata, 160
        Spicy Prawn Stir-Fry, 151
        Spring Tuna Niçoise Salad, 185
        Thai Tuna Salad, 189
        Tiger Prawn and Cauliflower Grits, 199
        Tuna Cakes with Rémoulade, 195
    Stage 1, 28–29
    Stage 2, 32–33
    Stage 3, 36–37
    Stage 4, 40–41
    Stage 5, 44–45
    Stage 6, 48–49
    Tex-Mex Pulled Pork Burritos, 152
    turkey
        Asian Braised Turkey Meatballs, 110
        Braised Tomato Sage Turkey Legs, 116
        Mexicali Turkey Burgers, 109
        Oven-Roasted Turkey Meatloaf, 138
        Turkey Reubens, 191
    vegetables
        Margherita Pizza, 194
        "Spaghetti" with Pomodoro Sauce, 136
        Winter Ratatouille, 113
Margherita Pizza, 194
meal planning, 24
    full diet, 52–53
    Stage 1, 28–29
    Stage 2, 32–33
    Stage 3, 36–37
    Stage 4, 40–41

Stage 5, 44–45
Stage 6, 48–49
Meat Stock, 58
meat, 15
  Stage 1, 27
  Stage 2, 31
  Stage 4, 39
Mexicali Turkey Burgers, 109
microbiome, 26
milestones, 54
Minced Beef Empanadas, 142
Minced Beef Stroganoff, 140
mind preparations, 20
Mini Butternut Squash Soufflés, 148
money-saving tips, 25
Moroccan Cauliflower "Couscous," 197
mouth, digestion functions, 10
mushrooms
  Aromatic Chicken with Mushrooms, 126
  Egg Drop Soup, 106
  Minced Beef Stroganoff, 140
  Pan Steak with Mushrooms, 102
  Warm Portobello, Red Pepper, and Basil Salad, 195

N
Nut Butter, 208
Nut Cheese, 209
Nut Milk, 71
nut-free recipes
  Apple Pie Stewed Apples, 154
  Aromatic Chicken with Mushrooms, 126
  Asian Braised Turkey Meatballs, 110
  Asparagus Fried Eggs, 122
  Beef Bone Broth, 60
  Beetroot and Beef Short Rib Borscht, 98
  Braised Beef Burgers, 108
  Braised Tomato Sage Turkey Legs, 116
  Butternut Squash Soup, 85
  Carrot Beet Soup, 86
  Cauliflower Hummus, 202
  Chicken Cheddar Sandwiches, 190
  Chicken Enchilada Casserole, 114
  Chicken Stock, 59
  Chicken-Stuffed Cabbage Rolls, 111
  Chicken Thigh Puttanesca, 163
  Chicken Vegetable Ratatouille, 112
  Chicken Vegetable Soup, 88
  Chopped Cobb Salad, 178
  Classic Chicken Soup, 84
  Classic Pot Roast with Onions, 139
  Creamy Tomato Soup, 96
  Cultured Spring Vegetables, 67
  Easy Avocado Omelette, 125
  Easy Chicken Stir-Fry, 151
  Egg Drop Soup, 106
  Fermented Mixed Vegetables, 66
  Garden Fresh Salsa, 203
  Garlic Chicken with Vegetables, 134
  Garlicky Greens Soup, 89
  Ghee, 70
  Gingered Vanilla Honey Drops, 169
  Grain-Free Tabbouleh, 147

Greek Lemon Vegetable Soup, 97
Green Goddess Juice, 132
Grilled Steak Salad, 181
Grilled Vegetable Frittata, 177
Guacamole, 150
Home-Churned Butter, 68
Honey Bombs, 168
Honey Sage Sausage Patties, 172
Kefir, 77
Kimchi, 200
Lemon Peppercorn Poached Chicken Breast, 101
Lemon Rosemary Salmon, 115
Liver-Loving Juice, 133
Margherita Pizza, 194
Meat Stock, 58
Minced Beef Stroganoff, 140
Mini Butternut Squash Soufflés, 148
Olive Raisin Tapenade, 162
Oven-Roasted Moroccan Chicken, 196
Pan Steak with Mushrooms, 102
Parmesan Rosemary Tuiles, 204
Pumpkin Bisque, 94
Santa Fe Breakfast Tostadas, 121
Sauerkraut Scramble, 120
Sausage, Egg, and Cheese Sandwich, 173
Scallops Piccata, 160
Seared Scallop Salad with Asian Vegetables, 182
Simple House Salad, 146
Slammin' Hot Slaw, 198
"Spaghetti" with Pomodoro Sauce, 136
Stewed Beef Porridge, 100
Summer Garden Soup, 92
Sweet-and-Sour Chicken Vegetable Soup, 90
Three-Onion Soup, 93
Tiger Prawn and Cauliflower Grits, 199
Vegetable Beef Stewp, 107
Very Berry "Ice Cream," 212
Wedge Salad with Ranch, 184
Yogurt, 74
nuts/seeds
  Almond Butter Honey Spread, 124
  Almond Flour Wraps, 153
  Almond Milk Yogurt, 75
  Baked Apples with Cinnamon, Walnuts, Raisins, and Yogurt, 155
  Baked Cinnamon Walnut Apples, 155
  Cherry Almond Chiller, 158
  Courgette Sunflower Cake with Currants, 210
  Crackling Nuts, 143
  Crackling Seeds, 143
  Everyday Grain-Free Bread, 78
  Flavoured Nut Milk, 71
  flours, 39
  Grainless Granola, 176
  Hunger Buster Bars, 211
  Nut Butter, 208
  Nut Cheese, 209

Nut Milk, 71
PB&J Smoothie, 158
Stage 6, 47
Three-Seed Crackers, 206
Walnut Pesto, 135

O
Olive Raisin Tapenade, 162
omega-3 fatty acids, 13
omelettes
  Easy Avocado Omelette, 125
  Salmon, Spinach, and Tomato Omelette with Avocado, 125
onions
  Classic Pot Roast with Onions, 139
  Slow Cooker Pot Roast with Onions, 139
  Three-Onion Soup, 93
Oven-Roasted Moroccan Chicken, 196
Oven-Roasted Turkey Meatloaf, 138

P–Q
Paleo diet-friendly recipes
  Apple Pie Stewed Apples, 154
  Aromatic Chicken with Mushrooms, 126
  Asian Braised Turkey Meatballs, 110
  Asparagus Fried Eggs, 122
  Beef Bone Broth, 60
  Beetroot and Beef Short Rib Borscht, 98
  Braised Beef Burgers, 108
  Braised Tomato Sage Turkey Legs, 116
  Butternut Squash Soup, 85
  Carrot Beetroot Soup, 86
  Cauliflower Hummus, 202
  Chicken Enchilada Casserole, 114
  Chicken Muffins, 131
  Chicken Stock, 59
  Chicken-Stuffed Cabbage Rolls, 111
  Chicken Thigh Puttanesca, 163
  Chicken Vegetable Ratatouille, 112
  Chopped Cobb Salad, 178
  Chunky Chicken Salad, 188
  Classic Chicken Soup, 84
  Classic Pot Roast with Onions, 139
  Crackling Nuts, 145
  Creamy Tomato Soup, 96
  Cultured Spring Vegetables, 67
  Dairy-Free Key Lime Mousse, 166
  Easy Avocado Omelette, 125
  Easy Chicken Stir-Fry, 151
  Egg Drop Soup, 106
  Everyday Grain-Free Bread, 78
  Fermented Mixed Vegetables, 66
  Garden Fresh Salsa, 203
  Garlic Chicken with Vegetables, 134
  Garlicky Greens Soup, 89
  Ginger Pumpkin Muffins, 130
  Gingered Vanilla Honey Drops, 169
  Grain-Free Tabbouleh, 147
  Grainless Granola, 176
  Greek Lemon Vegetable Soup, 97
  Green Goddess Juice, 132
  Grilled Salmon with Walnut Pesto, 135
  Grilled Vegetable Frittata, 177
  Guacamole, 150

Hunger Buster Bars, 211
Kimchi, 200
Lemon Rosemary Salmon, 115
Liver-Loving Juice, 133
Meat Stock, 58
Minced Beef Empanadas, 144
Nut Butter, 208
Nut Cheese, 209
Nut Milk, 71
Oven-Roasted Moroccan Chicken, 196
Oven-Roasted Turkey Meatloaf, 138
Pan Steak with Mushrooms, 102
Salmon Spinach Cobb Salad, 186
Santa Fe Breakfast Tostadas, 121
Sauerkraut Scramble, 120
Seared Scallop Salad with Asian Vegetables, 182
Seasonal Mixed-Berry Crostata, 166
Simple House Salad, 146
Slammin' Hot Slaw, 198
"Spaghetti" with Pomodoro Sauce, 136
Spiced Carrot Cake, 210
Stewed Beef Porridge, 100
Summer Garden Soup, 92
Sweet-and-Sour Chicken Vegetable Soup, 90
Tex-Mex Pulled Pork Burritos, 152
Three-Onion Soup, 93
Three-Seed Crackers, 206
Vegetable Beef Stewp, 107
Very Berry "Ice Cream", 212
Pan Steak with Mushrooms, 102
Parmesan Rosemary Tuiles, 204
PB&J Smoothie, 158
Peppery Pear Juice, 132
pesto
  Pesto Guacamole, 150
  Spinach Pesto Sauce, 137
  storing, 135
  walnut, 135
Philly Cheesesteak Pizza, 194
pizza, 194
planning ahead for the diet, 24–25
Pomodoro Sauce, 136
pork
  Honey Sage Sausage Patties, 172
  Sausage, Egg, and Cheese Sandwich, 173
  Sausage Gravy, 175
  Tex-Mex Pulled Pork Burritos, 152
poultry. See chicken; turkey
preparations
  kitchen/pantry, 22–23
  mind/body, 20
  planning ahead, 24–25
probiotics, 13
pumpkins
  Ginger Pumpkin Muffins, 130
  Pumpkin Bisque, 94
  Roasted Pumpkin Bisque, 95

R
raisins
  Baked Apples with Cinnamon, Walnuts, Raisins, and Yogurt, 155

Olive Raisin Tapenade, 162
raw ingredients
  honey, 169
  milk, 73
rebalance, five R's of gut healing, 13
Red Cabbage Kraut, 64
reinoculate, five R's of gut healing, 13
reintroducing dairy, 55
remove, five R's of gut healing, 12
repair, five R's of gut healing, 13
repeating the intro diet, 55
replace, five R's of gut healing, 12
Roasted Brussels Sprout Apple Salad, 159
Roasted Chicken Stock, 59
Roasted Aubergine Spread, 202
Roasted Pumpkin, 95
Roasted Pumpkin Bisque, 95
Roasted Vegetable Frittata, 177
Roasted Butternut Squash Pancakes, 124
Russian Dressing, 191

S
salads
  Calming Kale Salad, 180
  Chopped Cobb Salad, 178
  Chunky Chicken Salad, 188
  Garden Salad, 146
  Grain-Free Tabbouleh, 147
  Grilled Steak Salad, 181
  Roasted Brussels Sprout Apple Salad, 159
  Salmon Spinach Cobb Salad, 186
  Seared Scallop Salad with Asian Vegetables, 182
  Simple House Salad, 146
  Spring Tuna Niçoise Salad, 185
  Thai Tuna Salad, 189
  Wedge Salad with Ranch, 184
salmon
  Grilled Salmon with Walnut Pesto, 135
  Lemon and Rosemary Butter-Poached Salmon, 115
  Lemon Rosemary Salmon, 115
  Salmon, Spinach, and Tomato Omelette with Avocado, 125
  Salmon Spinach Cobb Salad, 186
sandwiches
  Chicken Cheddar Sandwiches, 190
  Chunky Chicken Salad, 188
  Italian Sausage Egg Sandwich, 173
  Lamb Burger Sliders, 192
  Sausage, Egg, and Cheese Sandwich, 173
  Tuna Cakes with Rémoulade, 195
  Turkey Reubens, 191
Santa Fe Breakfast Tostadas, 121
sauces
  Guacamole, 150
  Pesto Guacamole, 150
  Pomodoro Sauce, 136
  Spinach Pesto Sauce, 137
  Sun-Dried Guacamole, 150
  Tahini Lemon Sauce, 137
  Walnut Pesto, 135
Sauerkraut Scramble, 120

Sausage, Egg, and Cheese Sandwich, 173
Sausage Gravy, 175
seafood
  Fish Stock, 59
  prawns
    Tiger Prawn and Cauliflower Grits, 199
    Spicy Prawn Stir-Fry, 151
  salmon
    Grilled Salmon with Walnut Pesto, 135
    Lemon and Rosemary Butter-Poached Salmon, 115
    Lemon Rosemary Salmon, 115
    Salmon, Spinach, and Tomato Omelette with Avocado, 125
    Salmon Spinach Cobb Salad, 186
  scallops
    Scallops Piccata, 160
    Seared Scallop Salad with Asian Vegetables, 182
  tuna
    Spring Tuna Niçoise Salad, 185
    Thai Tuna Salad, 189
    Tuna Cakes with Rémoulade, 195
Seared Scallop Salad with Asian Vegetables, 182
Seasonal Mixed-Berry Crostata, 166
seasonings, 31, 42
seeds. See nuts/seeds
sensitivity testing, 34, 55
side dishes. See also snacks
  Cheddar Chive Biscuits, 174
  vegetables
    Butternut Squash Gnocchi, 141
    Cauliflower Mash, 103
    Chopped Cobb Salad, 178
    Garden Salad, 146
    Grain-Free Tabbouleh, 147
    Moroccan Cauliflower "Couscous", 197
    Simple House Salad, 146
    Simple Roasted Root Vegetables, 127
    Warm Portobello, Red Pepper, and Basil Salad, 195
Simple House Salad, 146
Simple Roasted Root Vegetables, 127
Simple Sauerkraut, 62–63
skin issues, 18
Slammin' Hot Slaw, 198
Slow Cooker Beetroot and Beef Short Rib Borscht, 99
Slow Cooker Pot Roast with Onions, 139
small intestines, 11, 18
snacks. See also side dishes; desserts
  Almond Milk Yogurt, 75
  Cauliflower Hummus, 202
  Coconut Milk Kefir, 77
  Coconut Milk Yogurt, 75
  Crackling Nuts, 143
  Crackling Seeds, 143
  Cultured Rainbow Vegetables, 67
  Cultured Root Vegetables, 67
  Cultured Spring Vegetables, 67
  Fermented Mixed Vegetables, 66
  Flavoured Kefir, 77

full diet, 52–53
Garden Fresh Salsa, 203
Ginger Pumpkin Muffins, 130
Grainless Granola, 176
Hunger Buster Bars, 211
Kefir, 77
Parmesan Rosemary Tuiles, 204
Stage 1, 28–29
Stage 2, 32–33
Stage 3, 36–37
Stage 4, 40–41
Stage 5, 44–45
Stage 6, 48–49
Three-Seed Crackers, 206
Tzatziki Sauce, 203
Yogurt, 74
soups
  beef
    Beef Bone Broth, 60
    Beetroot and Beef Short Rib Borscht, 98
    Slow Cooker Beetroot and Beef Short Rib Borscht, 99
    Stewed Beef Porridge, 100
    Sweet-and-Sour Beef Vegetable Soup, 91
    Vegetable Beef Stewp, 107
  chicken
    Chicken Bone Broth, 61
    Chicken Vegetable Ratatouille, 112
    Chicken Vegetable Soup, 88
    Classic Chicken Soup, 84
    Lemon Chicken "Rice" Soup, 84
    Sweet-and-Sour Chicken Vegetable Soup, 90
  Stage 2, 31
  stocks
    Chicken Stock, 59
    Fish Stock, 59
    Meat Stock, 58
    Roasted Chicken Stock, 59
    turkey, 117
  vegetable
    Butternut Squash Soup, 85
    Carrot Beetroot Soup, 86
    Chunky Butternut Kale Soup, 85
    Creamy Tomato Soup, 96
    Egg Drop Soup, 106
    Garlicky Greens Soup, 89
    Greek Lemon Vegetable Soup, 97
    Lemon Vegetable "Rice" Soup, 97
    Pumpkin Bisque, 94
    Roasted Pumpkin Bisque, 95
    Summer Garden Soup, 92
    Three-Onion Soup, 93
    Winter Garden Soup, 92
    Winter Ratatouille, 113
"Spaghetti" with Pomodoro Sauce, 136
Spiced Carrot Cake, 210
Spicy Chicken Enchilada Casserole, 114
Spicy Italian Chicken Sausage Patties, 172
Spicy Prawn Stir-Fry, 151
spinach
  Salmon, Spinach, and Tomato Omelette with Avocado, 125
  Spinach Pesto Sauce, 137
spiralizers, 23
spreads. See condiments

Spring Tuna Niçoise Salad, 185
squash
  Butternut Squash Gnocchi, 141
  Butternut Squash Purée, 149
  Butternut Squash Soup, 85
  Chunky Butternut Kale Soup, 85
  Mini Butternut Squash Soufflés, 148
  Roasted Butternut Squash Pancakes, 124
Stage 1
  overview, 26
  meats, 27
  recipes
    Beetroot and Beef Short Rib Borscht, 98
    Butternut Squash Soup, 85
    Carrot Beetroot Soup, 86
    Chicken Stock, 59
    Chicken Vegetable Soup, 88
    Chunky Butternut Kale Soup, 85
    Classic Chicken Soup, 84
    Creamy Tomato Soup, 96
    Crème Fraîche, 76
    Cultured Butter, 76
    Cultured Cream, 76
    Fermented Mixed Vegetables, 66
    Fish Stock, 59
    Garlicky Greens Soup, 89
    Greek Lemon Vegetable Soup, 97
    Kefir, 77
    Lemon Chicken "Rice" Soup, 84
    Lemon Peppercorn Poached Chicken Breast, 101
    Lemon Vegetable "Rice" Soup, 97
    Meat Stock, 58
    Pan Steak with Mushrooms, 102
    Pumpkin Bisque, 94
    Slow Cooker Beetroot and Beef Short Rib Borscht, 99
    Stewed Beef Porridge, 100
    Summer Garden Soup, 92
    Sweet-and-Sour Beef Vegetable Soup, 91
    Sweet-and-Sour Chicken Vegetable Soup, 90
    Three-Onion Soup, 93
    Winter Garden Soup, 92
    Yogurt, 74
  sample meal plan, 28–29
  tea, 27
  timing, 26
  vegetables, 27
  what you can eat, 27
Stage 2
  die off, 30
  expectations, 30–31
  recipes
    Asian Braised Turkey Meatballs, 110
    Braised Beef Burgers, 108
    Braised Tomato Sage Turkey Legs, 116
    Chicken Enchilada Casserole, 114
    Chicken-Stuffed Cabbage Rolls, 111
    Chicken Vegetable Ratatouille, 112
    Egg Drop Soup, 106
    Ghee, 70
    Home-Churned Butter, 68
    Home-Made Passata, 163
    Lemon Rosemary Salmon, 115

Mexicali Turkey Burgers, 109
Vegetable Beef Stewp, 107
Winter Ratatouille, 113
sample meal plan, 32–33
seasoning/spices, 31
what you can eat, 31
Stage 3
expectations, 34
healthy fats, 35
recipes
Almond Butter Honey Spread, 124
Almond Milk Yogurt, 75
Aromatic Chicken with Mushrooms, 126
Asparagus Fried Eggs, 122
Avocado Enchiladas, 114
Coconut Milk Yogurt, 75
Easy Avocado Omelette, 125
Red Cabbage Kraut, 64
Roasted Butternut Squash Pancakes, 124
Salmon, Spinach, and Tomato Omelette with Avocado, 125
Santa Fe Breakfast Tostadas, 121
Sauerkraut Scramble, 120
Simple Roasted Root Vegetables, 127
sample meal plan, 36–37
supplements, 34
what you can eat, 35
Stage 4
eating out, 38
expectations, 38
healthy fats, 39
recipes
Cauliflower Mash, 103
Chicken Muffins, 131
Classic Pot Roast with Onions, 139
Crackling Nuts, 143
Crackling Seeds, 143
Cultured Rainbow Vegetables, 67
Cultured Root Vegetables, 67
Cultured Spring Vegetables, 67
Everyday Grain-Free Bread, 78
Garlic Chicken with Vegetables, 134
Ginger Pumpkin Muffins, 130
Green Goddess Juice, 132
Grilled Salmon with Walnut Pesto, 135
Grilled Steak and Asparagus with Poached Eggs, 123
Home-Made Coconut Flour, 79
Lemon and Rosemary Butter-Poached Salmon, 115
Liver-Loving Juice, 133
Minced Beef Empanadas, 142
Minced Beef Stroganoff, 140
Nut Milk, 71
Oven-Roasted Turkey Meatloaf, 138
Peppery Pear Juice, 132
Roasted Chicken Stock, 59
Roasted Pumpkin, 95
Roasted Pumpkin Bisque, 95
Sausage Gravy, 175
Slow Cooker Pot Roast with Onions, 139
"Spaghetti" with Pomodoro Sauce, 136
Tahini Lemon Sauce, 137

sample meal plan, 40–41
supplements, 39
what you can eat, 39
Stage 5
expectations, 42
recipes
Almond Flour Wraps, 153
Apple Pie Stewed Apples, 154
Baked Cinnamon Walnut Apples, 155
Chamomile Ginger Apple Sauce, 154
Easy Chicken Stir-Fry, 151
Garden Salad, 146
Grain-Free Tabbouleh, 147
Guacamole, 150
Mini Butternut Squash Soufflés, 148
Simple House Salad, 146
Spicy Chicken Enchilada Casserole, 114
Sun-Dried Guacamole, 150
Tex-Mex Pulled Pork Burritos, 152
sample meal plan, 44–45
spices/seasonings, 42
what you can eat, 43
Stage 6
expectations, 46
recipes
Anytime Smoothie, 158
Cherry Almond Chiller, 158
Cherry Crostata, 167
Chicken Thigh Puttanesca, 163
Chocolate Honey Bombs, 168
Coconut Milk, 71
Coconut Milk Kefir, 77
Dairy-Free Key Lime Mousse, 166
Dairy-Free Raspberry Avocado Mousse, 167
Flavoured Kefir, 77
Gingered Vanilla Honey Drops, 169
Honey Bombs, 168
Olive Raisin Tapenade, 162
PB&J Smoothie, 158
Roasted Brussels Sprout Apple Salad, 159
Scallops Piccata, 160
Seasonal Mixed-Berry Crostata, 166
Sweet-and-Sour Red Slaw, 65
Thai Tuna Salad, 189
sample meal plan, 48–49
snacks, 48–49
what you can eat, 47
sterilization of dairy, 72
Stewed Beef Porridge, 100
stews. See soups
stocks, 14
Chicken Stock, 59
Fish Stock, 59
Meat Stock, 58
Roasted Chicken Stock, 59
stage 2, 31
turkey, 117
stomach digestion functions, 11
storing food, 25, 134
Summer Garden Soup, 92
Sun-Dried Guacamole, 150

supplements, 34, 39, 51
Sweet-and-Sour Beef Vegetable Soup, 91
Sweet-and-Sour Chicken Vegetable Soup, 90
Sweet-and-Sour Red Slaw, 65
sweetened foods, 47

T–U
Tahini Lemon Sauce, 137
tea, 27
testing foods, 54–55
Tex-Mex Pulled Pork Burritos, 152
Thai Tuna Salad, 189
Three-Onion Soup, 93
Three-Seed Crackers, 206
tomatoes
Braised Tomato Sage Turkey Legs, 116
Chicken Thigh Puttanesca, 163
Creamy Tomato Soup, 96
Garden Fresh Salsa, 203
Homemade Passata, 163
Pomodoro Sauce, 136
Salmon, Spinach, and Tomato Omelette with Avocado, 125
tuna
Spring Tuna Niçoise Salad, 185
Thai Tuna Salad, 189
Tuna Cakes with Rémoulade, 195
turkey
Asian Braised Turkey Meatballs, 110
Braised Tomato Sage Turkey Legs, 116
Mexicali Turkey Burgers, 109
Oven-Roasted Turkey Meatloaf, 138
stock, 117
Turkey Reubens, 191
Tzatziki Sauce, 203

V
Vegetable Beef Stewp, 107
vegetables
breakfast
Asparagus Fried Eggs, 122
Grilled Vegetable Frittata, 177
Mini Butternut Squash Soufflés, 148
Roasted Vegetable Frittata, 177
Roasted Butternut Squash Pancakes, 124
Salmon, Spinach, and Tomato Omelette with Avocado, 125
Santa Fe Breakfast Tostadas, 121
condiments
Cauliflower Hummus, 202
Garden Fresh Salsa, 203
Guacamole, 150
Olive Raisin Tapenade, 162
Pesto Guacamole, 150
Roasted Aubergine Spread, 202
culturing, 63
desserts
Courgette Sunflower Cake with Currants, 210
Spiced Carrot Cake, 210
fermenting, 15, 35, 62–63
full diet, 51

juices. See juices
main dishes
Chicken Muffins, 131
Chicken Vegetable Ratatouille, 112
Garlic Chicken with Vegetables, 134
"Spaghetti" with Pomodoro Sauce, 136
Winter Ratatouille, 113
salads. See salads
sauces
Pomodoro, 136
Spinach Pesto Sauce, 137
side dishes
Butternut Squash Gnocchi, 141
Creamy Coleslaw, 190
Cultured Rainbow Vegetables, 67
Cultured Root Vegetables, 67
Cultured Spring Vegetables, 67
Fermented Mixed Vegetables, 66
Kimchi, 200
Kowabunga Kimchi, 201
Moroccan Cauliflower "Couscous", 197
Red Cabbage Kraut, 64
Simple Roasted Root Vegetables, 127
Simple Sauerkraut, 62–63
Warm Portobello, Red Pepper, and Basil Salad, 195
soups
Butternut Squash Soup, 85
Carrot Beetroot Soup, 86
Chicken Vegetable Soup, 88
Chunky Butternut Kale Soup, 85
Creamy Tomato Soup, 96
Egg Drop Soup, 106
Garlicky Greens Soup, 89
Greek Lemon Vegetable Soup, 97
Lemon Vegetable "Rice" Soup, 97
Summer Garden Soup, 92
Sweet-and-Sour Beef Vegetable Soup, 91
Sweet-and-Sour Chicken Vegetable Soup, 90
Three-Onion Soup, 93
Vegetable Beef Stewp, 107
Winter Garden Soup, 92
Stage 1, 27
Stage 2, 31
Stage 3, 35
Stage 5, 43
Sun-Dried Guacamole, 150
Sweet-and-Sour Red Slaw, 65
Tzatziki Sauce, 203
Very Berry "Ice Cream," 212

W–Z
Warm Portobello, Red Pepper, and Basil Salad, 195
Wedge Salad with Ranch, 184
weight loss expectations, 18
wine, 51
Winter Garden Soup, 92
Winter Ratatouille, 113
yoga, 13
Yogurt, 74

Penguin
Random
House

DK US
Publisher Mike Sanders
Associate Publisher Billy Fields
Acquisitions Editor Lori Cates Hand
Development Editor Christy Wagner
Cover Designer Amy Keast
Book Designer Mandy Earey
Photographer Christopher Simpson
Food Stylist Laura Kinsey Dolph
Compositor Ayanna Lacey
Proofreader Amy Borrelli
Indexer Heather McNeill

DK UK
Editor Kate Berens
Project Editor Kathryn Meeker
Senior Art Editor Glenda Fisher
Managing Editor Stephanie Farrow
Managing Art Editor Christine Keilty
Senior Producer, Pre-production Tony Phipps
Senior Producer Stephanie McConnell
Creative Techical Support Sonia Charbonnier

First published in Great Britain in 2016 by
Dorling Kindersley Limited
80 Strand, London, WC2R 0RL

Copyright © 2016 Dorling Kindersley Limited
A Penguin Random House Company
10 9 8 7 6 5 4 3 2 1
001–290930–May/2016

A CIP catalogue record for this book
is available from the British Library.
ISBN: 978-0-2412-4829-4

Printed and bound in China.

All images © Dorling Kindersley Limited
For further information see: www.dkimages.com

A WORLD OF IDEAS:
SEE ALL THERE IS TO KNOW

ABOUT THE AUTHORS

Gavin Pritchard, RDN, CSSD, CD-N, CDE, is a nutritionist and health-supportive chef who has worked as an outpatient registered dietitian for more than a decade. Gavin has received advanced training in health-supportive cooking from the Culinary Institute of America in Hyde Park, is a board-certified sports specialist dietitian, and is a board-certified diabetes educator. He also has earned advanced certification as a health and fitness instructor from the American College of Sports Medicine and taken training in adult, childhood, and adolescent weight management.

Maya Gangadharan, NTP, is a certified nutritional therapy practitioner concentrating on gut health. Maya teaches classes on nutrition and presents kitchen demonstrations on making probiotic foods and beverages at Detroit's Eastern Market Community Kitchen. She has a clinical practice in Detroit and blogs at sohelpmegut.com.

ACKNOWLEDGMENTS

I would like to sincerely thank Maya Gangadharan for her passion, knowledge, and collaboration; Lori Cates Hand and the team at DK for their expertise and support; Marilyn Allen for her superb guidance and encouragement; and my amazing wife Maura and our two incredible daughters, Claire and Mari, for their patience, inspiration, and love.
—Gavin

I would like to sincerely thank Lori Cates Hand, Gavin Pritchard, and the team at DK for all their work, guidance, and support. Extra thanks to Magda Pecsenye for making the introduction. Much love and thanks to my mother, Mary, who taught me all about healthy, home-cooked meals, and to Rev, who always believes in me. Finally, to my amazing NTA instructors Caroline Barringer, Janelle Johnson Grove, and Christie Banners, and all my Ann Arbor 2015 NTP classmates and group leaders—thanks for having my back and teaching me so much. We've got this! —Maya

Special thanks to Courtney Rinehold, RDN, CDN, CLT, and her clients for testing the recipes.

PHOTO CREDITS

All images © Dorling Kindersley

10 Zygote Media Group, 12 Kristan Raines, 13 John Freeman, 18 Ruth Jenkinson, 21 Andy Crawford, 22 Dave King, 23 David Murray, Ian O'Leary, William Reavell, Dave King, Ian O'Leary, 38 Andy Crawford, 42 Roger Dixon, David Murray, 43 John Freeman, 46 Stuart West, 46 Lorenzo Vecchia, 47 Dave King, Chris Villano, 59 Stuart West, 62–63 Ali Donzé, 66 Dave King, 67 Steve Shott, 71 Lorenzo Vecchia, 72–73 Ali Donzé, 75 Dave King, 84 Will Heap, 85 William Reavell, 88 Dave King, 89 Steve Gorton, 92 Will Heap, 93 Dave King, 96 Dave King, 97 Will Heap, 99 Roger Phillips, 100 Andy Crawford, 106 David Murray, 107 Clive Streeter, 110 Dave King, 111 William Reavell, 114 Ian O'Leary, 115 Steve Gorton, 117 Philip Wilkins, 120 Claire Cordier, 124 David Murray and Jules Selmes, 125 Dave King, 130 David Murray, 131 Roger Dixon, 134 William Reavell, 135 Ian O'Leary, 139 Geoff Dann, 143 Andy Crawford, 146 Steve Gorton, 149 Roger Dixon, 150 Will Heap, 151 Roger Dixon, 155 Roger Dixon, 159 Peter Anderson, 162 Roger Dixon, 163 William Reavell, 165 Dave King, 167 Chris Villano, 168 Steve Gorton, 172 Lorenzo Vecchia, 176 Andy Crawford, 177 Roger Dixon, 180 Gary Ombler, 181 William Reavell, 184 Dave King, 185 Roger Dixon, 190 Gary Ombler, 194 Will Heap, 199 Roger Dixon, 202 Lorenzo Vecchia, 210 William Reavel, Roger Dixon. Divider pages: Dave King, Roger Dixon, Tim Ridley, Lorenzo Vecchia, Steve Gorton.